W9-DAY-634

THE PARA-PROFESSIONAL IN THE TREATMENT OF ALCOHOLISM

Third Printing

THE PARA-PROFESSIONAL
IN THE TREATMENT
OF ALCOHOLISM

[A New Profession]

Edited By

GEORGE E. STAUB, B.A., M.S.

Director
Alcohol Abuse and Alcoholism Program
Los Angeles County Department of Health Services
Los Angeles, California

and

LEONA M. KENT

Information-Education Officer
San Joaquin County Alcoholism Program
Stockton, California

CHARLES C THOMAS · PUBLISHER
Springfield · Illinois · U.S.A.

Published and Distributed Throughout the World by
CHARLES C THOMAS ● PUBLISHER
Bannerstone House
301-327 East Lawrence Avenue, Springfield, Illinois, U.S.A.

This book is protected by copyright. No part of it
may be reproduced in any manner without
written permission from the publisher.

© *1973, by* CHARLES C THOMAS ● PUBLISHER

ISBN 0-398-02860-5

Library of Congress Catalog Card Number: 73-5518

First Printing, 1973
Second Printing, 1976
Third Printing, 1979

With THOMAS BOOKS *careful attention is given to all details of manufacturing and design. It is the Publisher's desire to present books that are satisfactory as to their physical qualities and artistic possibilities and appropriate for their particular use.* THOMAS BOOKS *will be true to those laws of quality that assure a good name and good will.*

Printed in the United States of America
R-1

Library of Congress Cataloging in Publication Data

Staub, George E.
    The para-professional in the treatment of
alcoholism.

    1. Alcoholism--Treatment--Addresses, essays,
lectures. I. Kent, Leona M., joint author.
II. Title. [DNLM: 1. Alcoholism--Therapy.
2. Allied health personnel. WM 274 S798p 1973]
HV5275.S7   362.2′92   73-5518
ISBN 0-398-02860-5

821572

LIBRARY
ALMA COLLEGE
ALMA, MICHIGAN

To Bill Wilson
who started it all

CONTRIBUTORS

Fox, Vernelle, M.D.; Chief Physician of Alcoholism Services, Long Beach General Hospital, Long Beach, California; Coordinator of Alcohol Programs, University of Southern California School of Medicine, Los Angeles, California.

Kent, Leona M.; Education Information Officer, San Joaquin County Alcoholism Program, Alcoholic Rehabilitation Center, Stockton, California.

Keyes, Richard D.; Community Development Specialist, Alcoholism Training Program, University of California Extension/ Santa Cruz, Santa Cruz, California.

Kite, W. Richard, Ph.D.; Director of Alcoholism Training Program, University of California Extension/Santa Cruz.

Mann, Marty; Founder, The National Council on Alcoholism, New York, New York.

Maxwell, Milton, Ph.D.; Professor of Sociology, Center of Alcohol Studies; Executive Director, Summer School of Alcohol Studies, Rutgers University, New Brunswick, New Jersey.

McInerney, James, C.S.W.; Chief Counselor, Rehabilitation Center for Alcoholism, Lutheran General Hospital, Park Ridge, Illinois.

Pattison, E. Mansell, M.D.; Associate Professor, Department of Psychiatry and Human Behavior, University of California, Irvine, California; Deputy Director, Training, Orange County Department of Mental Health, Santa Ana, California.

Root, Laura, M.S.W.; Co-Director, National Alcoholism Training Program for Professionals, Social Science Institute, Washington University, St. Louis, Missouri.

Staub, George E., M.S.; Director, Alcohol Abuse and Alcoholism Program, Los Angeles County Department of Health Services, Los Angeles, California.

Strachan, J. George, F.R.S.A.; Consultant on Alcoholism to the Attorney General, Province of Alberta, Edmonton, Alberta, Canada.

Weisman, Maxwell N., M.D.; Director, Division of Alcoholism Control, Maryland State Department of Health and Mental Hygiene, Baltimore, Maryland.

Public Information Committee, Alcoholics Anonymous, General Service Office, New York, New York.

PREFACE

We have long dreamed of bringing together in one volume the thoughts of many of our friends, prominent in the field of alcoholism, on a subject which has been heretofore neglected in alcohol literature. Outside of the famous Krystal-Moore debates, there has been little written about the para-professional's role in the treatment of the alcoholic and alcohol abuser.

Many of our colleagues, engaged in developing new programs for the treatment of alcoholics, have asked for information and guidance on the hiring and training of staff, particularly the para-professional.

The contributing authors have found themselves asking the same questions during their careers and in many instances their experience has provided them with some of the answers. It is their thoughts we bring to you in this book. We hope that you will find them as meaningful and inspiring as we have.

We have asked ourselves if we are clinging to old fashioned and outmoded ideas. Before you read this book, we feel you should know what our basic philosophy is.

We believe that people in the field of alcoholism and alcohol abuse ought to work with and learn from Alcoholics Anonymous and its members.

We believe that people in the field of alcoholism and alcohol abuse ought to learn as much as they can about alcoholism as a disease entity and about the alcoholic, his dynamics, character, personality traits and motivation.

We believe that the kind of people who work in the field of alcoholism and alcohol abuse is more important than the techniques they use. Further, we believe that people-oriented services are more beneficial than chemical, technical, and mechanical approaches.

We believe that people providing direct services to the

alcoholic ought to relate to the well side of the individual rather than the sick side.

We believe that the vast majority of alcoholics cannot return to normal drinking.

We believe that the alcoholic should be treated by people specifically trained in the field of alcoholism and alcohol abuse. Further, we do not believe the alcoholic should be treated in generalized programs for the mentally ill.

We believe that people working in the field of alcoholism and alcohol abuse should have chosen to be in that profession and not fallen heir to it through promotion, nor taken the job merely because it was available.

We believe that programs should be evaluated on how well alcoholics are being served and on how many are recovering rather than on how well the needs of the bureaucracy are being met.

The philosophy we believe in may be considered, by some, to be conservative and behind the times. There is a possibility, however, that it may be liberal and far reaching. It is for you, the reader, to make this judgment.

You may notice, as you read this collection of writings, that all of the contributors do not speak with one voice, yet they do speak with one heart, a heart filled with concern for the alcoholic and for the para-professional who serves him.

We make no attempt to follow the traditional pattern of editorial comment on each chapter. We would encourage you to read each chapter completely and arrive at your own summary and interpretation.

We deliberately do not define the term para-professional, for it is defined throughout the book. This book is, in fact, a definition of what the para-professional is and does, and to attempt a lexographic reduction would be to destroy the whole point of this effort.

THE EDITORS

ACKNOWLEDGMENTS

I T IS TRADITIONAL to acknowledge the intellectual and personal debts owed to those who have contributed to the creation of a book. This is a tradition which we warmly endorse.

We will depart from this tradition, however, in order to demonstrate the basic point of this volume. The debt here is owed not to the scholars, to physicians, to treatment personnel, but rather to those suffering from alcoholism who have taught all of us contributing to this book, that our efforts could make a difference.

Biographical Sketch

George E. Staub is a native Californian. He is a graduate of the California State University at San Francisco, where he received his *B.A.* degree in psychology and his *M.S.* in Rehabilitation Counseling. He has worked in the field of alcoholism both para-professionally and professionally. He began his career as a research assistant on a federally financed project at the San Francisco Salvation Army's Men's Social Service Center. In 1966, he joined the staff of the Sacramento Alcoholism Center where he held the positions of counselor, supervisor, and administrator. In 1970, he became the State Administrator of the California Alcoholism Program. In 1972, he left state service and is presently the Program Director of Alcohol Abuse and Alcoholism Programs for Los Angeles County's Department of Health Services, Los Angeles, California.

Biographical Sketch

Leona M. Kent was born and educated in Chicago, Illinois. She began her career in the field of alcoholism as a para-professional counselor at the Sacramento Alcoholism Center, Sacramento, California. In 1969, she became the Education-

Information Officer for California's state alcoholism program. In 1972, she left state service and now is the *Information-Education Officer* for the *San Joaquin County Alcoholism Program* in *Stockton, California.*

Prior to her para-professional and professional experiences in the field, Mrs. Kent was deeply involved in community and voluntary work. She has been a consultant to many state and national programs, lecturing widely on prevention and on her original concepts of Alcoholics Anonymous Training Groups.

CONTENTS

THE PARA-PROFESSIONAL IN THE TREATMENT OF ALCOHOLISM

CHAPTER I

ATTITUDE: KEY TO SUCCESSFUL TREATMENT

MARTY MANN

PARA-PROFESSIONALS WORKING in the field of alcoholism are overwhelmingly recovered alcoholics. Most of them credit their recovery to AA, some to the facility where they are currently working, an increasing number to a combination of both, and a few to still other forms of therapy. One thing they all share is their attitude toward sick alcoholics, whether those alcoholics are in treatment, approaching treatment, or in and out of treatment with their motivation barely showing. Their attitude even encompasses all those sick alcoholics *out there*, who have not yet appeared anywhere at all seeking help, some of whom are known to the recovered alcoholics, but who cannot yet be reached.

What is this attitude that I call the key to successful treatment? First, it is accepting of the other person just as he is, for exactly what he is. Second, it accords him the dignity of his humanity quite apart from his illness which may have buried that humanity deep out of sight. He is regarded as a person, in great trouble to be sure, but not a non-person for all that. Third, it offers him understanding and, as a result of that, compassion, or as many recovered alcoholics flatly put it, *love*. Finally, and perhaps most important of all, it exhibits faith, a belief that he too, this alcoholic whoever he may be, can and will recover.

3

There is nothing about this crucial attitude that need be, or is in fact, confined to recovered alcoholics. It is the attitude of many professionals both in and out of this field; it lies within the power of any human being, professional or otherwise, to achieve. But it has been sadly apparent for many years that far too many non-alcoholic professionals, and other people surrounding the alcoholic, do not have this attitude. They have instead a composite of opposites to the points enumerated above. They are condemning, and therefore often hostile. They are quick to blame the alcoholic for his condition and to see the horrors of the condition as the man. They unwittingly treat him as less than human because he is not as they are. They are contemptuous of his *weakness,* his failure to stand up to life. They are sometimes punitive, believing that what he really needs is *to be taught a lesson.* They do not understand him and so they do not really like him. And he knows it.

It has been said that alcoholics are like children and dogs; they do not hear what you say, they feel what you feel. Their nerve ends are as if extended out from the body; probing, feeling, responding, often unconsciously seeking the rejection they have become accustomed to getting, testing the counselor. The effective counselor, professional or para-professional, has to be aware of this and prepared to handle it without becoming angry or soft, threatening or over-permissive. Sympathetic firmness is essential without ever resorting to maudlin sympathy. Here the recovered alcoholic knows the score so well that he can rarely be *conned* by the alcoholic patient. Active alcoholics are the world's greatest *con artists,* even when they have voluntarily sought help. They often cannot help it. Their behavior patterns are so ingrained by the time they begin treatment that they fall back into them, however unwittingly, at the first threat (usually the first sign that the treatment is working). So the effort to con the counselor can be a sign of progress.

To recognize this and to keep trying, in spite of many such episodes, requires a great deal of patience. The trained professional usually has this quality or has acquired it in the course of his training. The recovered alcoholic who wants to enter this field usually does not, unless his recovery has been a particularly good one, or the recovery process has been going on for a considerable time, at least three to five years. This is one reason why para-professionals require training before they can become effective counselors. The alcoholic is notably an impatient person with the need for instant gratification very apparent. Overcoming this problem and developing patience takes time and often considerable assistance. The para-professional who has succeeded in this can make an exceptionally good counselor, for his understanding of the patient's problem is great and he will not withdraw his support regardless of maddening behavior and frustrating responses.

There is no question that dealing with alcoholics can be a maddening and thoroughly frustrating experience. Many professionals, otherwise competent and even adept at working with sick and troubled patients, cannot, or at least do not, stay in this field. Most new facilities have had the problem of high staff turnover during their first year or two, until the *right* people came along . . . and stayed.

It could be asked whether the professionals' own attitudes were at fault. What prevented them from feeling comfortable with this particular group of patients? Did they harbor deep-seated feelings of hostility or contempt or fear of which they themselves were unaware even when their discomfort in dealing with these patients became acute? When I talk to professional groups about alcoholism, I urge them to consider this field, for there is a great need for their services. I also urge them to question themselves deeply before making the decision. Many of them may have imbibed the old wrong attitudes in their childhood, with no conscious awareness of having them. I tell them to look in the mirror and be honest, for if they have any of the old attitudes, they will not be comfortable dealing with alcoholics, and they might do harm rather than good by trying. The least that can happen is that they will not be effective. The need for personnel is too great to waste time on replacing or weeding out those who do not belong in the field. There are many who do belong if they could be recruited.

The challenges and rewards of alcoholism treatment are great enough to attract many able professionals. Yet there remains a great shortage of personnel. When new facilities are planned there are always heavy raids on established treatment centers for staff. Professionals new to the field are also being recruited; their number has increased ten-fold in the past ten years, but there are not enough. It has been said that if *all* those trained in *all* the helping professions were to be pre-empted into alcoholism treatment, there would still not be enough to provide adequate services for America's nine million alcoholics.

This is not very different from the plight of other health fields. A recent advertisement appealingly signed *America's Doctors of Medicine*, stated "America has only 278,000 physicians taking care of patients. One of us for 818 of you." Comparable figures for social workers, clinical psychologists, nurses and trained counselors are not available; neither are the figures for clergymen trained in pastoral counseling who are playing an increasing role in this area. It is clear that something more is needed and the para-professional may well be the answer.

In the field of alcoholism the para-professional has been used since the establishment, in 1944, of the first Yale Plan alcoholism clinics at Hartford and New Haven, Connecticut. There, a few recovered alcoholics worked under the direction of the professional staff and were called counselors. This was successful enough so that the practice spread as other facilities were opened.

The field of alcoholism is not alone in using para-professionals; the entire health field is turning to this as a solution to their major problem of manpower shortage. Alcoholism is unique in having available an immense pool of people (recovered alcoholics) who are willing and eager to serve as paid personnel or even as volunteers in treatment facilities. These are dedicated people, often highly intelligent and capable of learning new concepts quickly from their professional mentors. Increasingly, many of them are seeking out training opportunities to qualify themselves for entering the field. Fortunately, the number of training opportunities are increasing.

Meanwhile, many facilities take these people on, giving them on-the-job training. This has often proven very successful, but it can also present problems. The difficulty of selecting those best fitted for this work from a large number of applicants is very great. Certain qualifications have been widely used, most particularly the requirement of two years continuous sobriety. While this is a reasonable requirement, and greatly lessens the possibility of a relapse, it also creates quite a different hazard. A number of AA members with long years of unbroken sobriety (from ten up to twenty-five years) have proven unable to adjust to the problems of working in a professional setting, or to accept necessary professional supervision of their work. Their loyalty to their own method of recovery, that is, Alcoholics Anonymous, is so great that they cannot see the real value of professional methods and techniques. Of course, there are those who have shown great flexibility and willingness to learn and have easily fitted into the professional team with mutual benefit, even when they have been old enough to have accumulated many years of sobriety. Unfortunately, this type of individual, who has out-grown the restrictions of *tunnel vision* regarding AA's sole right and ability to reach and help all alcoholics, cannot be picked out from a pile of written applications. An interview is required and the interviewer needs to be very wise in the ways of AA members if he is to make a good choice.

Many AA members genuinely believe that *only* an alcoholic can help an alcoholic, a myth that persists despite the splendid records of many doctors, psychologists, nurses, social workers and clergymen in this field. However, as more and more alcoholics are helped by professionals and guided into AA by these same professionals, the understanding of the AA groups they join is measurably increased. There is a growing appreciation within AA circles of the very real value of professional help, and the increasing number of AA members working in professional set-tings as para-professionals helps to build and cement this appreciation.

I look forward to the day when all alcoholism treatment facilities will use teams including para-professionals, particularly those with an AA background. Each group has much to learn from the other, and in my opinion an amalgam of all these varied experiences may well produce a therapeutic approach better than any we have had to date. If the natural attitudes of re- covered alcoholics toward sick or recovering alcoholics could come to be shared by all members of the therapeutic team, this would be assured.

CHAPTER II

A DIFFERENTIAL VIEW OF MANPOWER RESOURCES

E. MANSELL PATTISON, M.D.

T HIS CHAPTER WILL focus on some of the factors involved in the overall development of necessary manpower for expanded alcoholism services in the United States. In addition, the field of alcoholism services has somewhat unique problems because of the various ideological positions assumed by different treatment programs, and reflected in varied professional and lay orientations. Therefore, we will illustrate how ideological orientations influence the choice and function of personnel, and how manpower can be differentially used to most benefit within each ideological treatment frame of reference.

AN OVERALL VIEW OF MANPOWER TRENDS

Although we are concerned here specifically with alcoholism manpower issues, and to some extent health manpower in general, the most salient steps in manpower development have been within the mental health field.[2, 10, 19]

In 1955, the Joint Commission for Mental Health and Illness undertook a national survey of mental health needs of the country. The manpower section, under the direction of George W. Albee,[1] produced a pessimistic report on the nation's capacity to recruit, train, and support the massive number of highly trained mental health professionals that would be required to provide mental health services to all levels of the populace. The Albee report

9

pointed out that extensive revision of the mental health care delivery system was required, so that manpower could be used more effectively and efficiently. The report called for a broader base of manpower, requiring less training, at a lower salary cost, and providing different types and methods of service.

In 1959, the method recommended for enlarging the manpower pool was to make more effective use of community personnel already engaged in human services not specifically involved in mental health. It was recommended that consultation and education programs be launched to make general physicians, nurses, ministers, probation officers, and welfare workers more effective as mental health agents who could provide case identification, referral, and some modest direct treatment.

Although a major national effort in consultation and education was launched, it failed to reduce the demand for traditional mental health personnel. There were various factors in that failure. One, the community agents were already overburdened in their existing roles. Two, many community agents were unwilling or unable to appropriately re-label their clientele as mental health problems. Three, a liaison with mental health personnel was rarely satisfactory, for the mental health professional tended to depreciate the skills, abilities, and contributions of community agents working within their own roles. Four, the development of community mental health services often failed to be innovative, but remained merely traditional systems for delivery of mental health care.

This manpower experiment did demonstrate, however, that many community agents, not specifically designated mental health personnel, did possess significant human helping skills, did successfully manage major mental health problems, and did provide a large volume of mental health services under other labels such as probation supervision, spiritual counseling, job counseling, and welfare management. Often community agents provided these services without explicit recognition of their mental health contributions.

A second experiment in manpower development was to train motivated laymen. For example, mature housewives were recruited for vocational mental health skill training. The notion was that such personnel with natural abilities and broad life experience could be successfully trained in specific mental health skills without formal professional training. Such projects were successful in that it was shown that housewives could indeed acquire adequate skills and knowledge and function effectively. The experiment was not successful as a manpower program. Most mental health programs would not hire these personnel because they lacked formal credentials, nor would most programs entrust them with primary patient care responsibilities because they were only *laymen*. Thus, the structure of the mental health system and the professional guild systems subverted this manpower experiment. The personnel were highly trained and highly effective, but they lacked professional credentials. Thus, this manpower experiment was evaluated not by skills and functions, but upon professional rites of passage. A third manpower experiment came out of the poverty programs of the early 1960's. It was recognized that the development of community mental health programs in poverty areas and minority ghettos was dependent on appropriate community involvement.

The involvement began with the recruitment and employment of community representatives, so-called *indigenous* community mental health workers. This had a three-fold rationale. One, these personnel were thought to be in close touch with their community, able to relate to their community, and hence more effective in meeting mental health needs of the community. Two, indigenous community personnel were sought as voices for their community to bridge the gap between the poor of the community and the affluent middle class mental health professionals. Three, recruitment of indigenous personnel was seen as a method for providing new jobs and new careers. It would enable the poor to ascend a ladder of access and success in the middle class world of professional mental health work.

The indigenous community worker experiment has had varied success over the past ten years, but overall has achieved marginal success. One, the indigenous workers quickly became identified with the world of professional mental health, leaving behind the mores, styles, ideologies, and values of their home communities. Two, the role of liaison or ombudsman was difficult if not, impossible to maintain. Either the indigenous worker joined the mental health ideology and system of bureaucracy, or he maintained a community identification and loyalty, often becoming provacateurs and militant employees leading protests and revolts against the mental health establishment that employed them. Three, this was not a truly new career, for rarely was a personnel career ladder established. Most were employed as entry level workers, and they had no further opportunity for advancement without resigning their jobs to take formal professional schooling. Nor, was their work looked upon as a professional, but rather as a non-professional or para-professional, who was clearly at the bottom of the professional pecking order. Most mental health programs employing the indigenous community worker did not change their patterns of utilization of personnel, nor change their methods of delivery of services.

The indigenous community worker experiment did demonstrate, however, that where given the opportunity, such workers could provide new and different services from those given by middle class professionals. They could provide more effective contact and entree into non-middle-class communities, and, given appropriate training and support, they could function effectively as primary care agents.

The fourth manpower movement has centered in the development of the volunteer mental health worker. The clinical use of volunteers was tested out in the volunteer staffing of suicide prevention and crisis intervention centers. It was found that non-professional volunteers were often more effective than mental health professionals. The volunteers were more practical, would easily relate to the crisis, and respond with meaningful human contact, whereas, the professional would remain more aloof, analytical, and less spontaneous. Similar experiences have been reported in the development of free clinics, walk-in centers, rap-groups, and other informal community programs where the emphasis is on casual human interaction, rather than on professional encounter and professional care-taking. At the same time, many formal mental health programs now use volunteers as initial contact workers, case-aides, history-takers, and other human assistance type services.[7]

These experiences with volunteers has shown that much of the work in mental health programs can be effectively performed by other than professional personnel, indeed providing needed care and services that mental health professionals did not or could not provide.

A fifth manpower experiment emerging only in the past five years, has been the *para-professional* movement. These programs typically are based upon relatively short term professional and academic training, aimed to produce a generic human services worker, able to deliver journeyman mental health skills, with modest schooling, relatively modest salary, and with personnel recruited from and serving their local community.

The para-professional movement has thus far enjoyed rather considerable success, with over one hundred junior colleges offering a two year Associate of Arts degree in human services work. These degree programs combine some basic liberal arts, technical mental health courses, and practicum work experience. An alternative model is the *new careers* programs, in which instance the workers are first hired in a human services agency, provided in-service training, and provided released time and educational support to obtain their Associate of Arts degree in an affiliated junior college.

Under either option, the intent is to avoid the problems of the previous manpower experiments. One, they aim to recruit personnel who will identify with the mental health program and professional patterns of care. Two, they build a base of professional preparation both academically and clinically. Three, they require a specifically created career ladder that provides for realistic career development. Four, they require specification and elaboration of clearly defined roles and functions in a mental health program. Five, career development for both employment and promotion gives recognition and credit for life experience, personal acquired skills, and community abilities. On the job and in-service training is aimed toward specific skill acquisition, not further formal education and recruitment into one of the traditional mental health disciplines. Six, despite the term para-professional, many of these programs now emphasize that these personnel are providing direct care and assuming major professional responsibilities. Therefore, they are now defined as *professional mental health workers.* The first level professional then is already defined within the professional ethos and has the opportunity to work upward in professional mental health ranks on the basis of acquired skills and knowledge.[19]

These developments in the expansion of the mental health manpower pool have important implications for the already existing mental health professional categories. It has been amply demonstrated that at the doctoral level of preparation, and certainly in terms of line-level function, the content and practice of those in clinical psychology, psychiatric nursing, clinical pastoral counseling, social work, and graduate psychiatry are highly similar. Thus, at the top level of mental health professional development we have parallel but almost similar personnel. Thus, education of professional mental health personnel is beginning to polarize. There is de-emphasis and a movement to eradicate the middle level professional, represented by the B.A. and M.A. level social worker, psychologist, and nurse. These disciplines are moving toward the preparation of large numbers of mental health personnel at the two year Associate of Arts level. This of course, coincides with what has been the independent development of Associate of Arts level generic human services workers. The major difference thus far has been the motive and method of recruitment. The discipline oriented programs have been recruiting personnel from the white middle class and white working class, whereas the Associate of Arts generic human services programs have emphasized recruitment of the poor, disadvantaged and minorities. In some programs, we see the merger of these two recruitment emphases.

Similarly, at the doctoral level, there is serious discussion of merging the various disciplines, amalgamating doctoral training into a single new mental health professional doctorate—for example, a doctorate in applied human behavioral science.

Thus, these partly speculative developments presage a move toward a continuum of mental health professional manpower. At the entry level of the professional ladder would be personnel recruited from the communities who would work and simultaneously acquire Associate of Arts level credentials, while some of their counterparts would first attend junior college before employment. These personnel would form the basic contact and treatment manpower pool. They will have modest degrees of initial formal training and education, with intermittent continuing education. They will acquire highly specialized skills within a relatively narrow range of functions, they will be professionals, but not scientists. They will be recruited and promoted in terms of personal skills and abilities, and demonstrated clinical capacities on the job.

In contrast, there will be small numbers of doctoral level personnel, functioning as specialists in human behavior. They may be recruited for academic training from the exceptionally skilled in the manpower pool, and from pre-doctoral programs including undergraduate nursing, psychology, medicine, and mental health curricula. This personnel will be scientists as well as professionals. They will provide little direct care, except that calling for highly refined technical skills. They will function as teachers, supervisors, consultants, researchers, program development and administrative specialists.

This discussion of directions in the development of mental health manpower indicates that we not only must recruit and train manpower, we must, also, look at the manner of delivery of mental health services and manner in which different types of manpower are utilized. At present, there is a high degree of *role diffusion*, that is, in many community mental health programs, all personnel do many of the same tasks without differentiation of skill, interest, or ability. What differentiation that does occur tends to be in terms of formal professional credentials, rather than upon personal demonstration of competence.

There will be at least three different *classes* of manpower. The *volunteer*, the *para-professional*, and a *continuum of professionals*.

The volunteer will provide a range of services, from purely personal services like transportation, to impersonal technical services, such as art or vocational instruction, to personal human interactions like telephone hot-line services or rap-group leaders. The volunteer differs from the professional in several significant respects. First, the volunteer tends to view the client or patient in terms of the common sense perceptions of the community. Thus, the volunteer will more likely identify with how the client or patient views the world. Second, the volunteer is not bound in his actions by the programs he serves, for if he disagrees he can leave. Third, the volunteer is not given sanction to make autonomous decisions with regard to the care and services to a client-patient. Fourth, the volunteer is not responsible, in a bureaucratic sense, for the care and welfare of the client-patient. That responsibility is incumbent upon the professional staff and the program administration. Thus, the volunteer may serve the system, but is not an integral part of the system. This may give the volunteer freedom and opportunity, but it also precludes major degrees of responsibility and requires sanction, support, and supervision from the responsible professionals.[7, 11, 12]

The para-professional may be considered as partly in and partly out of the professional program. The para-professional may be an aide, a technician, an assistant, or a person with program management responsibility. A para-professional does not have the societal sanctions, supports, ethics, and responsibilities that are both the blessing and bane of the professional. If a para-professional works in a professional organization, he has less status, power, authority, and responsibility. If a para-professional works in the community, runs his own program, etc. he is operating in somewhat of a no-man's land, for neither laymen nor professionals will typically perceive of this person as a professional operating a professional program. Indeed, at times it may be advantageous to remain outside the professional domain, and hence the independent para-professional program may be an important element of a total community program.[9, 11, 19]

The continuum of professionals which we have already discussed is predicated on the notion that each person designated as a professional is operating in terms of both the informal and formal structure of professional behavior. This includes a conceptual view of human behavior informed by the corpus of scientific knowledge, a sanction for autonomous and personal decision making, ethical and professional responsibility for client care and welfare, and identification with a peer group of fellow professional personnel. Thus, by professional we refer to conceptual orientation, a functional definition of working behavior, and sociological frame of identification. It does not refer to particular disciplines *per se,* to particular skills, or to specific diplomas or degrees. These latter are concrete results of professionalization, not the cause.

We anticipate that any comprehensive community mental health program will embody personnel of all three classes. Sometimes all within one organization, and sometimes in separate organizations that complement each other in terms of the total social system of community service.

MANPOWER FOR ALCOHOLISM SERVICES

Although the prior discussion has focused on mental health manpower, the same general issues are applicable to the field of alcoholism. There are, however, some major differences that merit separate discussion.

First, the field of alcoholism services has been ignored by health professionals in general, and mental health professionals in particular. Repeated surveys of professional agencies and professional attitudes indicate that there is a general negativistic attitude toward alcoholics, that generic service agencies ignore or screen out alcoholics, much less make measured efforts to make their services available to them, and that professionals both avoid choosing services to alcoholics as a professional option and avoid those who seek services in their agencies.[3, 4, 9, 18]

The result has been a curious and perhaps tragic vacuum. For the major bulk of alcoholism services manpower have come from the ranks of volunteers and para-professional personnel. Until at least 1950, the vast bulk of alcoholism programs and services were non-professional in nature. As Cahn[4] has documented, what professional alcoholism services were developed tended to be staffed by second class professional staff, with second class funding, resulting in second class professional programs operating in the back-waters of the main stream of professional developments.

Second, the training of mental health professionals has rarely included much preparation in the field of alcoholism.[6] Hence, professional recruitment has been difficult. Perhaps the bulk of professional recruits have been those who have been alcoholic themselves, achieved sobriety, and then sought professional training to return to the field of their personal experience. The influence of this type of professional has not been critically evaluated.

One response to this professional vacuum has been the development of specialized professional training programs for *alcoholism counselors.* These range from new careers training of recovered alcoholics to B.A. and M.A. level academic curricula. Although, such programs are personally successful, we must question their overall national value if they continue apart from a more general manpower development program. Such specialized alcoholism personnel would have little lateral mobility into other human services jobs, they would have little vertical mobility except on an idiosyncratic basis within a specific program, and they have ambiguous professional status and sanction at this time. On the other hand, if such professional training programs do interdigitate with more general manpower training and manpower personnel series, they could offer a highly potent specialized manpower development track for personnel directed toward alcoholism services.

Third, a major problem in the development of manpower, from a professional point of view, is the fragmented professional orientation towards alcoholism. We shall discuss this later, but it should be noted that some medical professionals view alcoholism solely as a biological problem, some psychiatric professionals view alcoholism solely as a neurotic emotional problem, some psychological professionals view alcoholism solely as a conditioned behavioral problem, etc. In sum, there is no widely accepted professional frame of reference within which professional training can be developed. Hence we have *partisan professionalism* rather than *scientific professionals.* Until a more adequate professional conceptual base for manpower preparation is developed, we may expect difficulties in the recruitment and training of adequate manpower.[5, 13, 18, 19, 22]

Manpower development in the field of alcoholism has been as spotty as that in mental health. There is the same admixture of volunteers, para-professionals, new professionals, and sundrie professionals. And in the field of alcoholism, this admixture is further confounded by various ideologies that inform the different types of alcoholism services.

MODELS OF ALCOHOLISM

Before we can discuss the discriminate utilization of manpower, we must look at the various delivery systems for alcoholism services. It is widely recognized that there are many different types of alcoholics, with different types of needs. Therefore, recent surveys of community planning programs have emphasized that communities establish multiple treatment programs that can provide a broad range of treatments based on population selectivity. These recommendations are based in the assumption that various treatment methods will be maximized by selecting the treatment approach most appropriate for specific types of alcoholics.[3, 18]

This concept of multiple treatment programs has been subject to a variety of misinterpretations, however. One misinterpretation is the shotgun approach. It provides a number of different treatment methods in one facility in the hope that something will take. Another misinterpretation has been the *competitive monolithic* approach, namely, multiple facilities in a community each offer its treatment as *the* way to treat all alcoholics—to the exclusion of other methods.

Neither of the above approaches to multiple treatment programs provides a sound conceptual and scientific base for comprehensive program planning or manpower utilization. The alternative is a model of *multiple complementary* programs. An analogy may illustrate this model. Each community has a number of places where one may purchase alcohol. One is a grocery store, another a cheap walk-in bar, another a posh night club. Different people seeking alcohol go to a different place, for they seek not just alcohol—but associated rewards and interactions associated with drinking alcohol. In the same way, different people seeking help for their alcoholism will select the treatment program that is congruent with their definitions of alcoholism, their view of their problem, and what types of associated interactions they see as involved in the help-seeking process. Becoming an alcoholic involves selective choices of community agencies (bars, etc.) and rehabilitation likewise involves selective choice. So our overall task is to develop matching facilities and programs that meet the perceptual and definitional needs of various sub-sets of alcoholics.[15, 16, 17]

To illustrate this process of matching, I shall give vignettes from a recent study of four different types of alcoholism treatment facilities.[17] These vignettes will illustrate how the alcoholics who voluntarily sought treatment at each of these four facilities represent four very different types of alcoholism sub-populations. Each facility uses very different treatment methods, to achieve very different treatment goals. And each facility (and the alcoholics who go to each) define alcoholism in a different manner.

The Aversion Conditioning Hospital

This population has the highest education (college), has achieved the highest socio-economic status, has maintained intact marriages, has the healthiest interpersonal and vocational health scores. These are all indicators of capacity for successful social competence. MMPI data indicates a constellation of personality traits requisite for social skills, for they are oriented toward social acceptance, externalization of problems, somatization of anxiety. In other words, these people are able to successfully keep life conflict outside themselves, or at least out of conscious conflict. They seek a treatment program that will restore flagging social acceptance, are sensitive to social sanctions, and they turn to appropriate social resources.

This population of alcoholics is relatively less sick, hence have less need for, or room for, improvement in total life rehabilitation. Alcoholism for them is still seen as an external problem. Alcoholism has not severely disrupted their social and vocational life. If these people feel that they have reached their most desparate point, that level is not nearly as low as for alcoholics at the other facilities. These are *high bottom* alcoholics. Further, being socially sensitive they may seek treatment earlier in their career of alcoholism before disintegration has occurred, with more social and vocational pressures present to push them into treatment. Although, they have been drinking as long as the alcoholics at other facilities they appear to have more capacity to defend against overt alcoholism.

For this population alcoholism is a disease, a medical problem akin to heart trouble or a broken leg, not a reflection of personal conflict. The medical view of alcoholism is a psychodynamic and sociodynamic stance that allows them to maintain their characteristic life style.

The facility in turn reflects the needs and perceptions of this population. The population is *high class* and the treatment is *high priced.* The medical orientation of the hospital conveys the message that medical personnel will do something to the person to rid him of the unpleasant affliction, alcoholism. The aversion treatment philosophy allows the subjects to maintain their image of adequate, successful individuals. Further, this facility does little in the way of social and vocational rehabilitation, since little is needed in this area. Nor does it provide much psychological treatment. Overtly, this facility does not define alcoholism as a psychological problem. Yet the facility would probably be less successful if it did attempt psychological treatment, for such would challenge the major defense systems of this population.

The Alcoholism Outpatient Clinic

This population provides evidence of less social competence. They have a high school education, have more middle class jobs, have married but experience more divorces, have intermediate interpersonal and vocational health scores. The MMPI data indicate a capacity for moderate defenses against anxiety, but not sufficient to prevent breakthrough of anger, depression, and feelings of inadequacy and passivity. This population experiences conflict while still maintaining a reasonable degree of social competence. They are still socially sensitive and look to socially respectable resources, however, they are more negativistic and pessimistic.

They see alcoholism as a personal problem, yet fear that it will overwhelm their lives more than it has. The definition of alcoholism as an expression of neurotic conflict is an apt summation of their personal experience of being alcoholic. In this population there is less need to maintain status by using a medical rationalization like the Aversion Hospital alcoholics do. Yet alcoholism is disrupting their lives and hence undercuts their capacity to deny that alcoholism is a personal problem.

The outpatient clinic is the most eclectic of the facilities. It has a physician and nurse to manage withdrawal symptoms. Disulfiram and psychotropic drugs are prescribed, and patients are informed of and encouraged to attend Alcoholics Anonymous. Yet the main modality is psychotherapy. Treatment is addressed to the personal conflicts that cause the patient to abuse alcohol, and to deal with the consequences of drinking in order to provide insight and strengthen ego adaptive skills. These alcoholics do not seek dramatic life rehabilitation, but they cannot afford to *close over* and deny the personal nature of their alcoholism. This facility does not provide shelter and life maintenance for this population still can maintain social competence. Nor does this facility focus on abstinence as its treatment goal, since the supposition is that symptomatic alcoholism will disappear with the resolution of life conflict. This is a feasible treatment approach for this population. In contrast, abstinence must be a treatment goal for the Aversion Hospital alcoholics since life conflict is maintained outside awareness; whereas in the subsequent two facilities to be discussed abstinence is required because they lack sufficient social competence to go ahead with the business of living life while simultaneously coping with their drinking style, abstinence for them is a precursor to rehabilitation.

The Alcoholism Half-Way House

This population demonstrates the effects of diminished social competence. They have only partial high school education, have held laboring and technical jobs, have mostly suffered marital disintegration, and have less healthy interpersonal and vocational health scores. Their MMPI data show character traits of inability to cope adequately with conflict and stress. They seek succorance, anger is repressed in the service of getting others to help them, and manipulation of others to provide for them becomes a major coping style in their lives. They experience a breakdown of coping mechanisms and turn to others, the clergy, institutions, to rehabilitate them.

These are the *low bottom* alcoholics. They possessed enough social competence to achieve a degree of successful social adaptation before alcoholism caught up with them. They have suffered huge steps downward from their previous jobs and family relationships. Although not on skid road they are close to it. Alcoholism for this population is not an isolated affliction, but a major disruption of their entire life. The use of the medical model of alcoholism is not a defense this population can use. Even if they stopped drinking immediately they would still face immense problems of social and vocational rehabilitation. Neither can they employ the model of alcoholism as a neurosis, for alcoholism is a total life problem, not just a neurotic affliction. Further the psychological *set* of this population would not fit them for the usual methods of middle class psychotherapy, for they are faced with the real life exigencies of just existing. Alcoholism is a problem of life, a need to start over, a spiritual renewal, a destruction of the self which means that a new style of life adaptation must be carved out.

The half-way house facility reflects the definitions and needs of this population. There is heavy reliance on Alcoholics Anonymous philosophy, including the need to surrender one's previous life style, to start over, to begin to live one day at a time, the quasi-religious conversion to becoming a new man. The AA philosophy emphasizes the need to change one's whole orientation toward life and towards one's self, and this matches very well the fact that alcoholism has destroyed their lives and a major reconstruction of a pattern of living is needed. Similarly, the program does not emphasize denial, nor strengthening of ego skills to dispatch neurosis. Rather, it starts by providing nurturance, gratification of daily needs and desires, it sets limits and defines behavior, very necessary for persons with limited ego strength. The facility provides a setting for re-socialization, and only secondarily is psychological enquiry made. This is social rehabilitation, followed by vocational rehabilitation.

The Police Farm Work Center

This population lies at the lowest end of the social competence scale. These men are the socially inept. They only completed grade school, have held transient laboring jobs, have usually never married. Their interpersonal and vocational health scores are the unhealthiest. Their MMPI data reveal a lack of capacity to cope with stress. They show little capacity to deal with internal conflict save via direct action. Hence, they show psychopathic qualities, non-conformity, overt hostility, yet despair and depression. There is little strength in themselves which they can call upon, hence they can only look to external agencies and personnel to cope with life. Alcoholism is for them just another piece of problematic behavior with which they cannot cope. They see little difference between treatment methods of facilities. They have no hope that life can be different. Their only goal is to achieve some respite in life by living in an institution that will provide them with support and nurturance that they cannot give themselves. They will pass from one institution to the next. Within an institution that provides necessary supports they can function, outside a supportive institution they cannot.

The facility provides a program that in actuality meets the immediate needs of this population, although the treatment goals of the facility may be more ambitious than appropriate. The subjects live in the work farm for sixty days isolated from society and from liquor. The subjects are provided with guided and supervised living experiences, and some realistic work experience is provided. It is the type of facility, were it a long term domiciliary, that might provide a sheltered living base where this population might function at a modest level of self-care. The facility makes no major effort at gradual social re-entry, it does not provide significant psychological counseling. It may perceive these areas as desirable additions to the program, but these additions would doubtless be of little value to the recipients. In contrast to the Half-Way House alcoholics where the problem was *re-socialization,* the problem here is *primary socialization,* which would also require significant augmentation of basic psychological coping skills, basic vocational training, and entry into society. The facility provides a short term drying out and a brief surcease from the buffeting rounds of skid road life, which may be the appropriate level of intervention for this population.

The Manpower—Facility Match

Although the vignettes do not cover all possible types of treatment programs or facilities, they are different enough to indicate how the model of alcoholism plays a role in the types of problems that must be met, the methods required, and the need for different staffing patterns.

To look at the matter another way, there are at least five different areas of alcoholism rehabilitation: 1) improvement in drinking behavior *per se;* 2) improvement in interpersonal social function; 3) improvement in internal psychological emotional function; 4) management of acute physical and chronic medical complications of alcoholism; 5) improvement in vocational capacity and function. Not all alcoholics are imparted in each area. Nor are all alcoholics imparted to the same degree in each area. Further, some treatment programs are designed to achieve improvement in one area or another, but not necessarily in all areas. Finally, different manpower with different skills are required to help rehabilitate the alcoholic in each area of rehabilitation.

As one illustration of these relationships, Table I, lists the possible manpower implications for just the four facilities discussed. In the overall development of manpower for the field of alcoholism we will need to develop a much more comprehensive scheme, in which specific types of personnel, with specific orientations, with specific skills, will provide specific service functions, in specific treatment programs.

TABLE I

EXAMPLES OF MANPOWER-FACILITY MATCH

Facility	Aversion Hospital	Outpatient Clinic	Half-Way House	Police Farm
Definition of Alcoholism	medical allergy	neurotic symptom	life problem	secondary nuisance
Treatment Goals	abstinence	emotional restructure	new life style	stay dry and sober
Treatment Methods	aversion conditioning	psychotherapy	group socialization milieu	sheltered structured living
Staffing	1. medical professional 2. technical aides	1. mental health professional 2. technical aides 3. community counselors	1. para-professional 2. volunteers	1. para-professional

UNIQUE ALCOHOLISM MANPOWER

Although other chapters in this book describe a variety of manpower, it is important to look at the unique issues of relationships between personnel recruited into alcoholism services.

Alcoholics Anonymous

One of the most misunderstood groups of personnel are the members of AA who have been lonely pioneers. At times the AA movement has been seen as the only manpower resource in the field of alcoholism. Yet AA has also been disparaged as non-professional or even anti-professional.

These views overlook the social psychology of all self-help groups. Hans Toch,[20] in his extensive study of non-professional self-help movements has found that there are certain universal characteristics. One, self-help movements arise when professional helpers do not provide effective services. Two, therefore, the deviant distressed people turn to each other for help. Three, they discover that they can help themselves. Four, because they can help themselves they conclude that professionals cannot help them. Five, because they have developed an effective self-help method they conclude that their method can help anyone similarly afflicted. Six, they conclude that their method is effective, and if a person fails in their system, it is the failure of the person not the system. Seven, their self-developed conceptual interpretation of the deviant problem is correct, as proved by the efficacy of their self-help method.

Now it is important to note that all self-help groups have an intrinsic anti-professional bias, have a non-science based conceptual frame of reference, and a self-fulfilling prophecy justification of their method. All of these ingredients are necessary for a self-help group. These attitudes are the social glue that coalesce such groups, and promote the group solidarity and commitment that make them successful.

It is important *not* to attempt to *scientificize* or *professionalize* a self-help movement. The mode of collaboration with mutual respect for differing methods and differing concepts allows both the self-help movement efforts and professional efforts to exist side by side and complement each other. In line with our discussion thus far, Alcoholics Anonymous provides a certain entree for certain types of alcoholics, whereas professional programs provide entree for other types of alcoholics. Both are part of an overall community system. But it would be a mistake to demand agreement on methods and concepts.

The Ex-Alcoholic as an Alcoholism Worker

In our initial discussion it was pointed out that one facet of manpower development was the recruitment of indigenous community workers, who both knew their community and were to be afforded a career providing escape from the poverty ghetto. The same motif is found in the recruitment of the indigenous recovered alcoholic. Certainly, it has been advantageous in providing workers who are familiar and comfortable in working in *alcoholism territory*. Wiseman[23] pointed out in her book on skid row, *Stations of the Lost,* recruitment into alcoholism programs as an alcoholism worker is indeed a method of career escape from the *alcoholism ghetto.*

The disadvantages are that rarely are new careers afforded the ex-alcoholic. He has a job and a career so long as he can trade on his expertise as an ex-alcoholic.[21] That card of expertise also limits him in terms of providing expertise in other areas of human service. There are exceptions, of course. The other major disadvantage is that the ex-alcoholic tends to operate within a limited frame of reference, an alcoholic's view of the world. He may therefore continue to function with many biases, prejudices, and distortions of the complex world of human services that may limit his effectiveness, or constrain the purview of his program.

The Ex-Alcoholic as a Professional

As noted, a number of ex-alcoholics have been recruited into professional ranks. Often they are dedicated and conscientious workers. They have often assumed positions of major leadership in the field of alcoholism. I have had the opportunity to train, supervise, and collaborate with many such professionals. On the basis of my personal observations, I conclude that they have made major contributions to the field of alcoholism.

On the other hand, the ex-alcoholic as a professional may sometimes work at a personal disadvantage. For example, the ex-alcoholic usually enters his professional training with relatively set views about alcoholism. He is not seeking professional training so much to learn about alcoholism as to acquire professional credentials. Hence, he may be disinterested in those aspects of professional training and knowledge that he does not see as pertinent to the field of alcoholism. Because of his personal investment in recovery, he may be emotionally resistant to professional knowledge that challenges his personal view of recovery and rehabilitation. And, finally, the most personal and poignant dimension may be that the ex-alcoholic is torn inside himself between a commitment to a view of alcoholism that undergirds his continuing personal stability and a commitment to intellectual and scientific knowledge and its concurrent professional integrity. As one professional told me: "When I work, I view alcoholism scientifically, but when I live, I view alcoholism the way I know I have to live."

The ex-alcoholic professional may bring certain insights, understandings, and compassion to the professional field, while at the same time he may have less personal freedom to look at alcoholism problems dispassionately and perhaps innovate new approaches.

The Culturally Indigenous Alcoholism Worker

In the past ten years, the mental health field has become painfully aware of the culture biases of our community mental health programs. Most mental health services have operated from white middle class biases. This problem, from my observations, is even more accentuated in alcoholism services.

For example, alcoholism is the number one health problem on the American Indian reservations. Yet most of the typical urban alcoholism services are inappropriate and ineffective when applied to Indian reservation programs. The successful Indian programs have relied upon indigenous Indian personnel from the local community on the reservation or in the urban Indian ghetto. The same holds true for alcoholism services located in black or chicano urban ghettos and barrios.

In recognition of this fact, recent urban programs have been developed that are based in ethnic communities, staffed by indigenous community personnel, with program structure geared to life styles and values systems of the community. One of the major manpower issues that faces the alcoholism field, is the recruitment, training, and effective utilization of minority personnel in appropriately designed service programs.

AN OVERVIEW

In this chapter we have outlined some of the major facets of the total manpower picture, in order to illuminate the picture within alcoholism services *per se.* In general, adequate manpower development requires careful attention to the recruitment of community personnel, the development of career personnel series with horizontal and vertical mobility, and the re-structure of delivery systems of care so that manpower can be deployed in terms of skills and functions rather than merely professional credentials. It is suggested that manpower development in alcoholism should be an integral part of the overall national mental health manpower scene.

We have given illustrations of different types of alcoholism service systems. Each system has very different characteristics and require different manpower staffing patterns. Goals of re-habilitation require different types of programs, staffed by different personnel with skills and knowledge.

And finally, the appropriate use of all manpower in the field of alcoholism must recognize the assets and liabilities of those personnel who are unique to the field of alcoholism.

The political battle cry *we need to attract more people into the field of alcoholism* is illusory. We will always need more personnel. Effective and appropriate deployment of personnel is quite another matter. The discriminate differential deployment of manpower is dependent upon the development of discriminate and differential methods of alcoholism services.

REFERENCES

1. Albee, G. W.: *Mental Health Manpower Trends.* New York, Basic Books, 1959.
2. Arnhoff, F. N.; Rubinstein, E. A., and Speisman, J. C.: *Manpower for Mental Health.* Chicago, Aldine, 1969.
3. Blum, E. M., and Blum, R. H.: *Alcoholism: Modern Psychological Approaches to Treatment.* San Francisco, Jossey-Bass, 1967.
4. Cahn, S.: *The Treatment of Alcoholics: An Evaluative Study.* New York, Oxford University Press, 1970.
5. Einstein, S., and Gecht, D.: What matter in treatment-relevant variables in alcoholism. *Int J Addictions,* 5:43, 1970.

6. Einstein, S., and Wolfson, E.: Alcoholism curricula: how professionals are trained. *Int J Addictions, 5:*295, 1970.
7. Ewalt, P. L.: *Mental Health Volunteers.* Springfield, Thomas, 1967.
8. Glasscote, R. M.; Plaut, T. P. A.; Hammersley, D. W.; O'Neill, F. J.; Chafetz, M. E., and Cumming, E.: *The Treatment of Alcoholism: A Study of Programs and Problems.* Washington, D.C., Joint Information Services, 1967.
9. Gottesfeld, H.; Rhee, C., and Parker, G.: A study of the role of paraprofessionals in community mental health. *Community Mental Health Journal, 6:*285, 1970.
10. Grosser, C.; Henry W. E., and Kelly, J. G.: *Nonprofessionals in the Human Services.* San Francisco, Jossey-Bass, 1969.
11. Hartog, J.: A classification of mental health non-professionals. *Mental Hygiene, 51:*517, 1967.
12. O'Donnell, E. J.: The professional volunteer versus the volunteer professional. *Community Mental Health Journal, 6:*236, 1970.
13. Pattison, E. M.: A critique of alcoholism treatment concepts; with special reference to abstinence. *Quar J Studies on Alcohol, 27:*49, 1966.
14. Pattison, E. M.: A critique of abstinence criteria in the treatment of alcoholism. *Int J Social Psychiatry, 14:*268, 1968.
15. Pattison, E. M.; Headley, E. B.; Gleser, G. C., and Gottschalk, L. A.: Abstinence and Normal Drinking: An assessment of changes in drinking patterns in alcoholics after treatment. *Quart J Studies on Alcohol, 29:*610, 1968.
16. Pattison, E. M.; Coe, R., and Rhodes, R. A.: Evaluation of alcoholism treatment: Comparison of three facilities. *Archives of General Psychiatry, 20:*478, 1969.
17. Pattison, E. M.; Coe, R., and Doerr, H. O.: Population variation between alcoholism treatment facilities. *Int J Addictions, 8:*199, 1973.
18. Plaut, T. F. A.: *Alcohol Problems: A Report to the Nation.* New York, Oxford University Press, 1967.
19. Sobey, R.: *The Non-professional Revolution in Mental Health.* New York, Columbia University Press, 1970.
20. Toch, H.: *The Social Psychology of Social Movements.* Indianapolis, Bobbs-Merrill, 1965.
21. Trice, H. M., and Roman, P. M.: Delabelling, relabelling, and alcoholics anonymous. *Soical Problems, 17:*538, 1970.
22. Verdon, P., and Shatterly, D.: Alcoholism research and resistance to understanding the compulsive drinker. *Mental Hygiene, 55:*331, 1971.
23. Wiseman, J.: *Stations of the Lost: The Treatment of Skid Row Alcoholics.* Englewood Cliffs, Prentice-Hall, 1970.

Chapter III

SYSTEMS DEVELOPMENT AND ROLE CHANGES NEEDED FOR ACCEPTANCE OF THE PARA-PROFESSIONAL IN AN ALCOHOLISM TREATMENT PROGRAM

Vernelle Fox, M.D.

T HIS CHAPTER DOES not attempt to speak to the vast potential contribution of the para-professional to the treatment of people with alcoholism. The author is concerned here with the changes needed in traditional delivery systems to make these contributions possible. Inherent in these systems changes are the problems of role definition of established staff to enable the inclusion of each other, as well as the para-professional. In order to speak to these problems the author's concepts of the disease process we are dealing with and some of the attitudes needed for successful treatment must be understood.

This chapter will attempt to provide an overview of alcohol dependency, the goals of treatment and structure of organization and leadership needed to allow the therapeutic elements of staff, situations and patients to become engaged in a process toward health. The chapter's message is that staff and patients need to openly and honestly communicate. They must find gratification in being part of something larger than themselves, with each solving life's problems without the need for total control over outcomes.

WHO IS QUALIFIED?

"Who is qualified to treat the alcoholic?" is a question frequently raised in the literature and more frequently brought up at various professional meetings. The question and ensuing discussions sometimes become quite heated and may deteriorate into an emotional hassle. People who are concerned with the care of the alcoholic usually develop their concern in one of two ways: a vested interest because their professional work has brought them in contact with alcoholism, or because of their personal encounter with the illness. In discussion they tend to polarize into *either-or* concepts. *Only professionals can treat patients, only recovered alcoholics can understand alcoholics.* Competitiveness and insecurity are a part in these discussions. *We have the answer. No, we have the answer.* It takes time for either group to become secure enough to appreciate the additive benefits of the utilization of both groups.

Actually alcoholism is such a huge and complex problem that all available, appropriately directed helpers need to join forces to develop as many and as broadly based approaches as possible.

We can no longer afford the luxury of comfortably sitting in our meetings and debating the subject of who should treat these patients. Since people with addictions represent a microcosm of almost all mankinds' physical, psychological and environmental problems it is imperative that we utilize all available techniques to help solve these problems. This means that a treatment program should consist of the coordinated efforts of concerned professionals and para-professionals with as wide a variety of skills as possible, working both within the program and out in the community. This is a noble philosophy but it has many inherent problems when put into effect.

Facility staffs are usually composed of individuals, as previously stated, who come to the service by way of vested interest either because of training in a helping discipline or because of personal involvement with the illness and its recovery process. Under either circumstance they are usually well trained in specific techniques, and accustomed to assuming unilateral responsibility for the patient or client. They have learned to measure their own success or failure by the patients' progress in a specific direction. This expectation is usually toward a value system more like their own and necessitates the patients finding a new identity and a meaningful life without chemicals.

In practice the patient's new identity is with his fellow patients. The staff to some degree are outsiders. They serve as a model, but are probably not the most important factors in the patient's recovery. No one staff member is central to a patient's progress. This means that the patient is not *in treatment* with anyone. He belongs to the program and all staff are responsible for contributing whatever they can to help the individual function in this framework and find his strength.

Every discipline or category of genuinely concerned people have a potentially significant input at the right time with the right patient. After all, at this point and with our current knowledge, we can only treat people with people.

The possible variations of specific potentially meaningful treatment sessions are as numerous as the mathematical product of the number of encounters between effective helpers and addicted patients seeking help. The key is not *who* should be working in alcoholism programs but *how* to more adequately utilize the potential of each individual who is capable of and willing to invest of themselves and their skills for these patients.

ADMINISTRATIVE LEADERSHIP

A major key to the successful development of an effective inter-disciplinary team is the administrative leadership. The individuals holding the ultimate administrative responsibility can make or break the entire effort. These persons must have sufficient strength to be able to make policy decisions and stand behind them in the face of open dissent and criticism. The only way to implement policy, in a therapeutic way, is to have the policies evolve from the bottom on a majority rules basis and then have administration be willing to back the policy which was actually set by patients and staff. A certain minority will use this as a vehicle to test their strength. If the administrator or leader is insecure in backing the decision of the group and needs to justify or prove his position, there will be continuous change and administrative policy or authority will be used by members of the team in their power struggle. When this happens the issues will always be clouded and individual struggles will never be faced and dealt with. The situation can deteriorate to one of pre-occupation with proving who has the power rather than finding ways to have one's ideas and philosophies incorporated into the whole. If communications are blocked, or even just allowed to not happen, some staff will ramrod their convictions under the guise of *they* want things done this way. The *they* is the implication of administrative backing. Other staff, either less aggressive or less articulate, will be reduced to feeling that their only power is a veto power. Consciously or unconsciously they will gradually develop an attitudinal set of *I'm not going to do it until they direct me to do it.* Since the *they* was implied authority backing in the first place, no direction comes. By this time, issues are usually so clouded that no one knows what is actually at stake. When this happens, nothing happens. That is, one portion of staff is busily trying to get the other portion to do it their way and the other portion is busily resisting, finding reasons not to do it their way. The inevitable result of this kind of stalemate is that staff are preoccupied with self and patients are lost in the process.

The kind of leadership needed to avoid this situation is an individual or small group who feel the support and backing of the ultimate funding body and who are willing to accept the responsibility if the large group is wrong. In practice this is not as formidable as it might sound. Groups have an amazing way of reaching sensible and practical conclusions once individual members have been given the opportunity to ventilate radical and/or hostile divergencies. Administrative leadership that allows for free expression of the team's in-fighting and listens, reasonably impartially, to all sides before reaching a decision and then is willing to assume the full responsibility for that decision, is quite likely to find itself with majority staff support and full backing for implementation. Tests of strength will always occur but programs will move forward and much will happen to allow those who were testing to find satisfaction in areas other than being in control.

This alone is an essential contribution of administration. In addition, the authority of administration, therapeutically used, can be a major contribution to not only the obvious need to do things differently, utilizing the talents of all kinds of people doing many kinds of untraditional things, but also to set and back up healthy and realistic limits for both staff and patients. This is a rather fine dividing line. To maintain this precarious balance for the influence to be therapeutic rather than a continuing obstacle, administration must be continuously involved in the day to day program, staff conferences, planning meetings, and all other staff activities.

THE TREATMENT PROGRAM

Some of the vital components of a comprehensive program include detoxification and physical restoration initially, and sometimes repeatedly. Environmental manipulation may often be indicated. Orientation and education as to how to use and benefit from a new peer group identity is essential. Continuing reinforcement and rewards for constructive participation, along with crisis intervention at any point, are mainstays of any treatment approach. A comprehensive program must also work with family, employers and significant others to help them encourage the patient's continued involvement and to reinforce appropriate behavior.

The medical management component of the program must be put first in terms of point of time in the patient's treatment schedule. The principles of medicine's contribution are fairly simple and sometimes easier to put together than other vital components.

While the medical phase is offered first to the patient it does *not* necessarily need to be the dominant or controlling facet of the overall program. It can be a relatively quiet or an understated aspect of the whole as long as it is readily available and properly coordinated with the other components. Because medicine's contribution is essential and because it is sometimes more acceptable to the patient, more promising of the magic, there is always the possibility of this becoming the focus of a power struggle. Physicians and nurses can use their control over patients as means of negating the contribution of other disciplines. Conversely, the behavioral scientists can band together to undercut the medical contribution. If either should happen it is essential that administration not be trapped into taking sides but take a firm stand that a total program must have all components and insist that the various factions spend enough time and effort to learn to communicate and work together in a way that directs their competitive energies toward giving the most to patients.

In the first place the patients are usually fragmented, isolated, and frightened. They have a well established identity of *I am a drinking problem*, not *I have a drinking problem* and tend to relate to others only by means of this drinking problem identity. It takes considerable time and effort on the part of the staff to help the patient develop a new peer group identity and begin to see themselves as *people* struggling with a drinking problem. They manipulate and divide their would-be helpers and have an amazing capacity to set the staff in competition with one another to assume the responsibility for solving the patients' drinking problem.

A major hurdle for newcomers in the field of alcoholism is the realization of the fact that making the patient stay sober is not the responsibility of the staff. Patients, families and others tend to see a relapse or return to drinking as a total failure of previous treatment efforts and have a need to fix the responsibility of blame on someone. New staff tend to accept this responsibility and become defensive. As this happens the patient begins to move back into the identity of being a drinking problem with which treatment people are coping instead of a person with a problem.

The choice between creative living and self-destruction is and must remain the prerogative and responsibility of the patient as it is with every other human being. The differences between this responsibility for choice of his life's direction in the course of treatment and the attitudes of *he got himself into it, therefore, let him get himself out* are subtle. It takes time and experience, and considerable inter-professional support, for staff to become comfortable in assuming their responsibility for giving of self to patients without the need to make them perform or behave in the way that society would desire.

THE TREATMENT STAFF MEMBERS

We use the words *staff members* in the broad sense that encompasses every person who contacts a patient in a particular setting. This means *every person* with whom the patient comes in contact: the telephone answerer, the medical director, the grounds-keeper, the AA member, the volunteer, the professional and the para-professional. The rest depends upon the pattern that the individual service follows. Actually, the list should not be restricted to people contact. The nature and location of the physical facility, the color of the walls, the dog who is the program's mascot, the admission's policy, hours of operation and a host of other factors have a vital input, creative or distructive as the case may be, into the total effect upon the patient or client and his significant others.

Since staff members are basically just people, they have many difficulties establishing and maintaining open and honest communications with fellow staff members trained in other disciplines and for other roles. This is anxiety provoking and involves a great deal of personal risk. Each must accept the fact that his own personal experience and concern alone, will not have a major impact on many patients. At the same time, he must not lose sight of the value of his potential contribution to the total program. This sets the stage for a great deal of competitiveness among staff. Keeping this competitiveness in the open and using it creatively is the major key to the success of the program. The staff's handling of these inter-relationships, their ability to find gratification in being part of what is important rather than having to be all of it or none of it, is the central problem. The staff's handling of these issues and the ability to find satisfaction in contributing and sharing serves as the model for the patient community. If a major goal of alcoholic rehabilitation is to train people to find satisfaction in living with people, instead of chemicals, we must help them give up their need for omnipotence and control. It is difficult, if not impossible, to teach or sell a concept that one has not learned or bought.

All staff must learn from each other. Individual staff members need a great deal of personal maturity and mutual trust to function in such a loose structure and with so little authoritative direction. Shared responsibility is vague and the yardstick for one's accomplishment is ill defined. Constant effort must be made to maintain open communication among the staff and to keep in focus the fact that the goal is to help set the stage to enable the patient to continue to be involved, not to *cure* him.

These aspects of staff interaction puts specific pressures upon the para-professional in the treatment team. The more established disciplines speak with some kind of authority and, if so endured, look down their professional noses at the para-professional who, in a given situation, may well know more about the individual patient or the specific details of a referral source. It is easy enough to say that the person with the most knowledge of the patient's need and the resources available to him should call the shots of what the patient should be exposed to over the years that constitute his recovery period. Good theory, but not too compatible with the old medical model. Who ever heard of a head nurse, rehabilitation counselor, social worker, to say nothing of a lay counselor working in this area, having more creative ideas about the recommendations for a patient than the traditional captain of the ship. This simply means that people must be willing to stand up and be counted.

To review, the enabler is not the curer. The team and program components need to be extensive and comprehensive, while being coordinated by team and administrative involvement and commitment to the treatment of those mutually searching for selfworth in ways other than by chemicals.

Much modification of our models needs to be done to allow, encourage and utilize the *people skills* of persons already on the team and others yet to come. The patients are our peers in treatment. At the end, the patient must become the doctor and share in health what he found while becoming well.

CHAPTER IV

IN-SERVICE TRAINING OF THE PARA-PROFESSIONAL IN THE FIELD OF ALCOHOLISM

LAURA ROOT

INTRODUCTION

FOR MANY YEARS para-professionals have been working in the field of alcoholism and have served in a variety of helping roles as suggested earlier in this book. Some have received on-the-job training, while still others may have taken a course or two at a university or an institute sponsored by a local council on alcoholism or perhaps attended one of the many summer schools of alcohol studies which are held annually in the United States. For many, however, little or no formal training has been given and they have had to learn from working with the alcoholic patient and/or from the professionals with whom they may work.

"There are many persons who fortunately seem to possess a healing and soothing understanding manner . . ." according to Dr. E. L. Bartz. Some, however, have intolerance, impatience and lack of information which disqualifies both the professional and the non-professional alike in the management of the alcoholic.[1] Therefore, in this chapter we will consider what is needed most to assist the para-professionals in learning to work with the alcoholic on an in-patient basis as well as to consider

---

[1] Bartz, Edward L.: Notes and Comments. *Quart J Studies on Alcohol,* 25:3, p. 351, 1964.

what training might be helpful to them in order to truly fulfill a total role in this area.

In-service training as a specific program for the para-professional is a necessity if they are going to render a much needed service to alcoholics as well as making the most of their abilities. Obviously, in this field in which there is a continuous growth in the incidence of alcoholism, both locally and nationally, there are not enough professonals nor para-professionals working with the alcoholic. Furthermore, use of the para-professionals in this field has never been fully explored.

STANDARDS OR CRITERIA

What then is needed in terms of recruitment, personal characteristics, attitudes and training for the para-professional? Does this mean that there are some prerequisites for this field? Shall it be limited to persons who have recovered from the problem of alcoholism with a number of years of sobriety? Or shall it also include individuals who have a desire to help the alcoholic and/or the problem drinker?

As a result of the author's own positive experience in working with and training para-professionals, a basic format or outline for their training has been designed. A curriculum must include certain facts about alcohol and alcoholism which can be taught together with their *on the job* training. Ideally, it is recommended that in-service training occur in a modified therapeutic community with a multi-disciplinary team of which the para-professional is a team member, as are the usual disciplines which generally are represented on the team. Experience gained in the early 1960's in an alcoholism inpatient facility located in a mental health center, established the importance of changing and upgrading the status of the para-professionals who became members of the team. "In the past, the roles of the physician, nurse, psychologist, social worker *et al.* have been stressed, whereas in this modified therapeutic community for alcoholics, the roles of . . . counselors, psychiatric aides, licensed practical nurses, assumed their rightful importance at last."[2] It was imperative in the interaction of the team of this alcoholism facility for the professionals to encourage and support the para-professionals in changing their status and roles. Reluctance was encountered on the part of those members who had been previously employed in the psychiatric section of the hospital, to give up their subordinate role and assume an equality with the other team members. The para-professionals were not the only ones who had some difficulty with their roles; so too did some of the professionals who were encountering this *equalitarian ethos* for the first time. "This was especially true of those persons who had an upward-mobility syndrome."[3] Thus, some of the professionals had to be helped to adjust to colleagues who, while not degreed, were also on the team while they fulfilled their roles as professionals. It was found that with the continued acceptance and encouragement of all the professionals on the team, that the para-professionals were able to overcome their hesitancy and uncertainty by taking their rightful place on the team as fully participating members as did the professionals.[4]

IMPORTANCE OF ATTITUDES

Much has been written about attitudes which must be present in those individuals who are to work with alcoholics, such as acceptance, understanding, tolerance, non-moralistic judgment, etc. Therefore, if they are to work effectively with alcoholics, trainees should hold positive, not negative, attitudes. This has been documented in the research done by Pittman and Sterne and published in their article, *Concept of Motivation*. The authors view specific types of attitudes held by some professionals

---

[2] Root, Laura E.: *Social Therapies in the Treatment of Alcoholics,* Chapter 11. David J. Pittman (ed.), *Alcoholism,* New York, Harper and Row, p. 146, 1967.

[3] Pittman, David J.: The open door: Sociology in an alcohol treatment facility. *Alcoholism,* New York, Harper and Row, p. 140, 1967.

[4] Supported (in part) by a Mental Health Grant (MI 567) from the National Institute of Mental Health, United States Public Health Service.

as a source of professional blockage in the treatment of alcoholics.[5]

It is the belief of the author that certain attitudes must also be present or else blockage will occur in the training process to the degree that the trainees will not effectively carry out learning etc., for their therapeutic role with the alcoholic. A number of studies have shown that the intellectual capacities, the importance of attitudes, personality and/or the effects of personal characteristics have had an impact upon learning, i.e., training. Studies done by Chadorkoff and Bailey support the importance of the effect of attitudes upon learning.[6] Bailey tested attitudes before and after training social workers in three agencies in New York and concluded that training *per se* is not enough. Attitudes, then, effect the learning and training experiences drastically.[7] It would seem that intellectual knowledge about alcoholism and techniques and procedures would not prove too effective for the paraprofessionals unless accompanied by their emotional acceptance.

ATTITUDES AND TRAINING

In an article published in the *Quarterly Journal of Studies on Alcohol* in the 1940's by Dwight Anderson concerning lay therapists' roles and the possible contributions which they could make in the future, he noted that this would be lessened severely unless those persons who were responsible for training could: 1) learn how to recruit them selectively, 2) learn how to train them, 3) and learn how to use them on a multi-disciplinary team.[8] Anderson pointed out "that what the layman, who is a recovered alcoholic, lacks in techniques and understanding can be

---

[5] Pittman, David J., and Sterne, Muriel W.: The concept of motivation: a source of institutional blockage in the treatment of alcoholics. *Quart J Studies on Alcohol, 26*:41-57, 1965.

[6] Chadorkoff, Bernard: Alcohol education in a psychiatric institute. *Quart J Studies on Alcohol, 30*:657-664, 1969.

Bailey, Margaret: Attitudes toward alcoholism before and after a training program for social caseworkers. *Quar J Studies on Alcohol, 31*:669-683, 1969.

[7] *Op. Cit.*: Bailey.

[8] Anderson, Dwight: The place of the lay therapist in the treatment of alcoholics. *Quar J Studies on Alcohol, 5*:257-266, 1944.

supplied by training and supported by continuous help and supervision. . . ."[9]

The author agrees with Anderson, knowing many recovered alcoholics who have made tremendous contributions in the field of alcoholism. Unfortunately, however, not all recovered alcoholics should be selected to work therapeutically with all alcoholic patients.

George Strachan, in his book *Alcoholism: Treatable Illness,* supports the view that "attitude, empathy, and technique are even more important than medication *et al.*" He also indicates that "some recovered alcoholics are unable to accept these factors *per se* and not only are they unsympathetic to alcoholic patients but are even intolerant of their drinking behavior which makes them useless as counselors."[10] The author agrees with Strachan that some alcoholics should not be involved in treatment, since some, not many but some, take the view that their experience with the disease, as it effected them, and their specific recovery makes them experts in knowing all about all other types of alcoholisms.

These types of recovered alcoholics tend to be somewhat dogmatic with the alcoholics who are trying to get well. They are impatient, as well as critical of the individual with whom they are working, and insist that the alcoholic struggling for recovery must follow their program, since it worked for them obviously it works for all alcoholics. They usually are very authoritarian and insist on giving advice to the patient. It is the author's experience, however, in working with recovered alcoholics who are para-professionals, that the majority of them are very capable of working with most alcoholics. It must, however, be stressed that there are a certain few who should not. Therefore, as part of the preliminary design of training, recruitment should be selective concerning the attitudes of all of the trainees.

This is equally true of the non-alcoholic trainee. They must

---

[9] *Ibid.*
[10] Strachan, J. George: *Alcoholism: Treatable Illness.* Vancouver, Mitchell Press Limited, p. 148, 279, 1968.

be selected on the basis of their attitudes as well. Should there be any strong negativism against drinking, alcohol, and alcoholism, they should be considered less than an ideal candidate in this field of endeavor. It is the author's belief that an instrument could be devised to pretest attitudes of the trainees in order to select out the candidates who could be considered as being most receptive to training in the field of alcoholism. It should be mentioned also that some trainees who seem on the surface to be either moralistic and/or negative towards the alcoholic should be closely screened before they are rejected for training, since there is the possibility that some may have only a misunderstanding and/or misinformation about alcoholism and alcoholics. They should not be lost to the field for lack of an adequate evaluation.

Bailey used an attitude test which was a refinement of an earlier instrument design by Pittman-Sterne in their study, *The Carousel*. She administered it before and after to a group of social workers who were given a thirty-hour training program in alcoholism.[11] It was concluded, as a result of their testing and training, that emotional acceptance as well as positive attitudes and beliefs towards alcoholics being treatable must accompany learning.

Bailey sought to find out what attitudes were held concerning the nature and etiology of alcoholism moralism, abstinence, insight, optimism-pessimism, treatment relationship, etc.[12] Pittman-Sterne in part of their study attempted to assess attitudes held by health and welfare personnel with regard to alcoholism and the alcoholic. They investigated five attitudinal dimensions, namely: orientation toward alcoholism as a disease; the role performance of the alcoholic patient or client relative to other patient or client groups; role performance of the alcoholic patient; optimism regarding the treatability of alcoholism and the necessity of motivation as a prerequisite for recovery from alcoholism.[13]

----

[11] *Op. Cit.*: Bailey, p. 671.

[12] *Op. Cit.*: Bailey, pp. 672-674.

[13] Pittman, David J., and Sterne, Muriel W.: The Carousel: Hospitals, Social Agencies, and the Alcoholic. Report presented to the Missouri Division of Health, St. Louis, Missouri, 1962. Appendix IIIA.

An example of the types of questions used by Bailey are as follows:

a) Agree or Disagree: Very little can be done to help the alcoholic solve his other problems until he just stops drinking.

b) Agree or Disagree: Alcoholism is primarily the result of a physiological disposition.[14]

An example of some of the Pittman-Sterne questions are as follows:

a) Agree or Disagree: Alcoholics relapse so often that it sometimes seems pointless to treat them.

b) Agree or Disagree: Only those who can tolerate work which is unusually discouraging and unrewarding can ever succeed with alcoholics.[15]

These examples of the questions utilized in both studies could be refined, i.e., modified to apply to the group of trainees as to age, sex, educational status, etc. This then would provide a basis or criterion for selectivity of the trainees. What is the important point is that the emphasis be placed on the quality of the trainee as opposed to quantity of trainees. The danger is present that because of need quality might be sacrificed for quantity which could result in poorer patient care.

RECRUITMENT

It would seem that the para-professional who is to work with alcoholics should be recruited carefully. They should believe that anyone who has an alcohol problem can recover, that it is indeed a treatable illness. Without these beliefs and positive attitudes, the para-professional could prove to be less effective in a therapeutic relationship, as does the professional who holds negative views.

More importantly, it is known that the negative attitudes toward alcoholism can effect training. In fact, in a study which was done by Belasco and Trice, they suggested that sometimes "training may bring to the surface an individual's fear con-

---

[14] *Op. Cit.*: Bailey, pp. 672-674.

[15] *Op. Cit.*: Pittman-Sterne, Appendix IB-1 Form D, page XXXIV.

cerning his own drinking and therefore constitutes a threat to his or her self concept. They might think . . . is it possible that I too could become an alcoholic?"[16]

Thus, in selecting trainees, recruitment should be concerned with attitudes toward alcoholism, self-awareness, stability, an ability to relate well to people, as well as having the ability to communicate. Training then should be able to supply the core of knowledge together with the appropriate techniques and procedures necessary for this field.

TRAINING

Important in designing an in-service training program is the how, where, when and the frequency aspects which must be decided. If training is to occur in an inpatient facility such as a unit in a mental health center, a state hospital, or a general hospital, the design must take into consideration not only the trainees but the location and length of the training, and especially whether it may be given within the unit setting without disturbing the patients' routine. In the experience of the author, training which has been given on the unit, either in an office or a day room, where a film projector and blackboard were available, together with necessary facilities for the trainees to sit at a round conference table, is the best location for an in-service training program. Training should be given within the trainee's working hours and they should be freed from duty to attend.

A combination of didactic lectures, film presentations, discussion groups, role playing, etc., can be utilized to present the content of the course. Trainees must do more than simply listen to a variety of disciplines expounded on various aspects of alcoholism. They should become involved in the learning experience. Obviously, certain knowledge about the disease must be given, but it is imperative that this not develop into simply *a rote*

---

[16] Belasco, J .A., and Trice, Harrison: Training as a Change, a Constructive Evaluation. *Selected Papers, 17th Annual Proceedings.* North American Association of Alcoholism Programs, Chicago, Illinois, pages 42047, 1967.

learning exercise. Rather, it must be a vital positive, two-way participation between the trainees and the teachers. Part of the method would utilize the group itself as a learning device in order that the trainees may understand the dynamics of their group experiences.

A schedule for training sequence should take a minimum of fifteen weeks, meeting for three hours weekly. This could be divided either on the basis of three days, one hour sessions or two day meetings for ninety minutes for each session which would provide time for the basic course material to be given. Trainees should work under supervision with various patients as well as have the responsibility of presenting their evaluation of some of the patients in staff meetings on the unit. They must be able to report on how they view the patient and his illness and their viewpoints concerning his life style, etc. The learning experience should incorporate the didactic material, work with patients, as well as interaction with the professional staff.

Before beginning the training curriculum for the trainees, we should explore with them what are some of their ideas, beliefs, etc., which they may have about the disease; this goes beyond their attitudes. It might be anticipated that both the alcoholic and non-alcoholic para-professional might accept some of the usual popular beliefs which are held about alcoholism. There is much myth and misinformation concerning the physiological effects of alcohol which usually originates either from ignorance or folk beliefs and tales which are passed on from generation to generation. People generally accept the oversimplification of social drinking functions in our society. Some few have a limited knowledge as well, of the pharmacological action of alcohol. Most odd generalizations are drawn from subjective impressions and/or experiences of alcohol related problems, such as:

1) All alcoholics are unable to hold jobs.
2) All alcoholics cannot be trusted.
3) All alcoholics are pathological liars.
4) All alcoholics are never responsible even when sober.

These beliefs or sayings, call them what you will, unfortunately are accepted by too many persons in our society.

This type of misinformation may be held by some of the recovered alcoholic trainees as well as the non-alcoholic ones, since they may have similar cultural backgrounds, social mores and customs which accept the myths and misinformation about the alcoholic and the many alcohol related problems. Furthermore, the traditional acceptance of the moralism aspect is often hidden under different guises but basically indicates a belief that alcoholism is truly a moral issue and what is really needed is emphasis on willpower to overcome any drinking problem. This moral attitude, as is generally known, is a moral and emotional overlay from the early days of the Protestant ethic and post-prohibition attitudes.

If we do not evaluate the present beliefs that the candidates for training hold, we would be superimposing the alcohol information upon inaccurate facts, with the end result being confusion. The trainees receptivity of true information about alcoholics and alcoholism could become distorted, providing a poor basis for the subsequent training which is to follow.

DESIGN OF PROGRAM

In designing this in-service training program, the basic core of knowledge needs to be assimilated by the trainees so that they may not only learn about the illness and its effects, but more importantly are better prepared to understand and work with various types of alcoholisms and its resulting related problems with the families, the institutions, as well as agencies and the other community resources. The course outline is as follows:

I. Introduction—design of program
   A. Orientation
      1. Historical Overview—use of beverage alcohol predates history. Stone vessels for beer drinking, hieroglyphics on Egyptian caves circa 1500 B.C. which gave a warning against drunkenness.
      2. Widespread use of beverage alcohol—customs/ mores i.e., colonial America temperance meant moderation while drunkenness was frowned upon.

For example, the 1619 Virginia legislature passed a law concerning drunkenness as follows:
  a. First intoxication, the individual was reproved privately by a minister.
  b. Second intoxication, he was reproved publicly, and
  c. Third intoxication, he was placed in the stocks for twelve hours and had to pay a fine.
B. Trace the change of the custom when temperance meant moderation in the early colonies; the change when temperance meant abstinence and resulted in the passage of the Volstead Act.
C. What is the place of beverage alcohol in today's society's customs and mores and the various functions of drinking in our culture?

II. Social—Cultural Factors
  A. Socio - economic - class/status
    1. Lower class
      a. Income, etc.
      b. Drinking practices
    2. Middle and upper class
      a. Income, etc.
      b. Drinking practices
  B. Ethnic/religious and abstinence groups
    1. Drinking beliefs for and against
  C. Age, sex, race, and education
  D. Attitudinal Factors—National and regional attitudes towards drinking mores/customs and public intoxication

III. Alcoholism Theories
  A. Etiology of alcoholism
    1. Disagreements over the causes
  B. Definition as a disease
    1. Arguments over the disease concept *vis a vis* a problem and/or symptoms etc.
    2. American Medical Association and World Health Organization definitions

    C. Alcoholism as social deviancy *vis a vis* the established norms of society

    D. Incidence, ecology

IV. Significant Factors Effecting the Individual

    A. Physiological aspects

        1. Alcohol and the human body

        2. Metabolism

        3. Physical effects

        4. Chronic alcoholism

        5. Nutrition

    B. Psychological and Sociological

        1. Impact upon the person, his emotions, personality traits

        2. The alcoholic and his family

    C. Socio-economic and law enforcement

        1. Effect upon job

        2. Effect upon industry

        3. Alcohol-related offender

        4. Highway safety

        5. Court and DWI programs

        6. Legislation

V. Patterns/Types

    A. Alcoholisms

        1. Jellinek's classification

        2. Cahalan's problem drinkers

        3. Others. Symptom, deviancy, etc.

    B. Phases—gamma

    C. Developmental

        1. Search for labels for alcoholics[17]

        2. Not personality[18]

        3. Environmental

VI. Institutions and Personnel

    A. Facilities

        1. In-patient

---

[17] Cahalan, Don: *The Problem Drinkers.* San Francisco, Jossey-Bass, Inc. pp. 10-11, 1970.

[18] *Ibid.*: p. 152.

       2. Out-patient
       3. Half-way Houses
       4. Private Hospitals
       5. Domiciliaries/Shelters/Missions
       6. Foster Homes

   B. Personnel
       1. Professionals
       2. Alcoholism Specialists
          a. Various disciplines
          b. Para-professionals
       3. Health/Welfare organizations
       4. Volunteers

   C. Alcoholics Anonymous/Al-Anon/Ala-Teen

VII. Treatments

   A. Types
       1. Emergency care of the acutely ill alcoholic
       2. Chemotherapy
       3. Aversion Therapy
       4. Behavior Modification
       5. Psychotherapy
       6. Therapeutic Community
       7. Individual Therapy
       8. Group Therapy
          a. Alcoholism group therapy
          b. Role playing
       9. Religious Experience
    10. Total Approach—Comprehensive

   B. Rehabilitation and Aftercare
       1. Employment and vocational counseling—testing
       2. Counseling
       3. Retraining
       4. Securing employment
       5. Maintaining contact with patient

   C. Community Resources
       1. Agencies—giving specific services for the alcoholic
       2. Agencies—giving adjunctive services for the alcoholic

D. Follow-up
    1. Continuance
        a. Periodic appointments
        b. Clinic and home visits on an as-needed basis
    2. Follow through period of five to seven years
        a. Follow-up contacts
        b. Evaluation of patient—recovery

This detailed course outline for in-service training of the para-professional in the field of alcoholism can be given as a complete sequence or modified to a shorter course if necessary in terms of personnel, time and money available in a given facility. However, it is in the best judgment of the author that it is advisable to include all the formation listed above. This provides a solid foundation for on-the-job training which is included.

SELF CONCEPT AND THERAPY

Earlier in this chapter it was suggested that an attitude test be administered to the trainees prior to the begining of the in-service training period in order that the best possible candidates be recruited. It is equally important to evaluate the effect of training upon the trainees. Therefore, the attitude test should be administered again at the end of the program. Furthermore, it is necessary for the trainees to learn about their own self concepts, self image, self awareness, self understanding, and self discipline, so that they are more capable of handling their feelings when working with the alcoholic.

It is important in counseling, both in individual and in group therapy, that the trainees have a true self awareness of what they are as a person, for to know yourself and to understand your strengths as well as weaknesses is a must in working with the alcoholic patient. The trainees can be taught to manage themselves, to feel secure in the knowledge of themselves which leads the individual trainee into becoming more comfortable within and with themselves. In understanding and feeling comfortable with themselves they then tend to cope with their everyday life tensions, anxieties, uneasiness and develop more self discipline. This aspect is important in their work with alcoholics, especially as previously mentioned, in individual counseling and group therapy. Honesty with oneself and with the patient is a must if the trainees are to be truly effective.

This awareness and understanding enables the trainees to have better conceptions of the roles they must play with their fellow professionals and other team members as well as with the patients. If the trainees are able to delineate and understand their various roles in the setting, they then will provide a better service to the alcoholic patient and make a contribution to the team as well as the facility. Thus they must be adequate not only as a team member, but as a counselor, as group leaders, etc.

Furthermore, in learning and understanding themselves, they develop as individuals who are able to be involved therapeutically with the alcoholic patient, both at the verbal and non-verbal levels. Much has been written about the ability of the recovered alcoholic as a counselor, indicating that he is the only person who can truly understand and work with the alcoholic successfully. For some, this is very true, having gone through their own horrendous experiences with alcoholism, it generally provides them with a greater understanding than someone who is not an alcoholic. Sympathy for the alcoholic as well as an awareness of what the alcoholic is currently suffering must be clearly perceived by the trainee. However, as previously noted, some alcoholics do have sympathetic understanding and are tolerant of their fellow alcoholics. The non-alcoholic trainees, through their awareness of self and training, are able to have empathy and can be sympathetically introspective with the alcoholic. To the degree that they are able to understand and project themselves into the alcoholic's mind and emotions, they then are able to be sympathetically introspective as well as empathetic to what the alcoholic is currently experiencing.

In working with the patient therapeutically, communication is both verbal and non-verbal. It is important to teach the trainees about body gestures and the significance of the fact that their body movements verify what is being said and thought. Failure could occur if the trainee's body gestures were obviously negating what they were saying. For example, eyebrows raised by trainees while they were being verbally reassuring to a relapsed alcoholic would be evidence for the patient of the insincerity of the trainees.

The alcoholic is an extremely perceptive patient and he is able to detect insincerity immediately and quite typically withdraws into himself. Trainees must be helped in learning how to use themselves appropriately as they are learning their other roles during this training program.

EVALUATION OF TRAINEES—USE OF SELF

Following this rather intensive course, evaluation of the trainees reaction to the total program, other than the attitude test, should be made. What type of self image do they have following the training? Do they find that there were any areas of difficulty which they did not bring up during their training sequence? Do they perhaps see an improvement in their self images as a result of the training? Do they know themselves better? Do they tend to feel more comfortable with themselves now as a result of their training experiences?

These are some of the questions that should be discussed with the trainees as they finish the course. The basic curriculum, if it is given to the trainees over the recommended fifteen week period, should include some additional time devoted to rap sessions and/or discussion groups. This gives them an opportunity to explore their feelings and reactions to the course *per se*. In addition to the evaluation of their self concepts, it is suggested that the trainees be encouraged to react to what their negative as well as positive experiences were during the training. This is the time to ascertain if the trainees are strongly motivated to accept the challenge of working in this field before they commit themselves finally.

CONCLUSION

Quality must be stressed in recruiting and training the paraprofessionals. This should not be sacrificed for quantity because of the great need for people to work in alcoholism programs.

This point cannot be overemphasized because in the past the anxiety to obtain help to care for the alcoholic caused recruitment procedures to be less than selective.

A properly trained para-professional has much to give the alcoholic, not only on an in-patient basis but more importantly and even perhaps more effectively, in the area of aftercare and follow up. The potential use for the para-professional in this area has never fully been explored other than in Alcoholics Anonymous' Twelve Step work and in the field of mental health. Recently, an article in a national weekly newspaper about community psychiatry indicated that for decades volunteers have helped the mentally ill.[19] It is only in recent years, however, that they have begun to move out into community psychiatry. Dr. Francis Sobey, a professor of social work at Columbia University found in a survey which she recently completed, "that over 10,000 nonprofessionals, including volunteers and paid staff, were working in 185 mental health projects . . ."[20] The article goes on to describe the variety of roles being played by the volunteer especially in the area of aftercare. The author should like to raise the question, "Why not use the para-professional in the field of alcoholism, where aftercare has not been stressed too strongly, other than by Alcoholics Anonymous?" It is the author's belief that many para-professionals would be professionally capable of this task.

Follow-up could include office and/or home visits as well as having the para-professional available to the patient on an *as needed* basis. Furthermore, they could act as liaison between the in-patient or out-patient facilities and community agencies which provide rehabilitative services for the alcoholic. Many times it is desirable that someone follow through on how the patient is doing with a given agency. It is not an unknown phenomenon to have an alcoholic patient lost during a referral for lack of adequate and appropriate referral and follow-up.

---

[19] Driscall, James G.: Community psychiatry. *The National Observer.* 10:1, No. 32, Copyright Dow Jones and Company, Inc., Maryland, August 19, 1971.

[20] *Ibid.*

The para-professionals can be an effective force in the field of alcoholism if they are given the opportunities and accept the task. However, this cannot be done unless those of us who are responsible for recruitment and training learn, as Dwight Anderson said many years ago, "How to recruit selectively, how to train them, and how to use them appropriately . . ."

REFERENCES

1. Bartz, Edward L.: Notes and comments. *Quart J Studies on Alcohol,* 25:3, 1964.
2. Root, Laura E.: Social Therapies in the Treatment of Alcoholics, Chapter 11. David J. Pittman (ed.), *Alcoholism,* New York, Harper and Row, 1967.
3. Pittman, David J.: The Open Door: Sociology in an Alcohol Treatment Facility. *Alcoholism,* New York, Harper and Row, 1967.
4. Supported (in part) by a Mental Health Grant (MI 567) from the National Institute of Mental Health, United States Public Health Service.
5. Pittman, David J., and Sterne, Muriel W.: The concept of motivation: a source of institutional blockage in the treatment of alcoholics. *Quar J Studies on Alcohol,* 26:41-57, 1965.
6. Chadorkoff, Bernard: Alcohol education in a psychiatric institute. *Quar J Studies on Alcohol,* 30:657-664, 1969.
   Bailey, Margaret: Attitudes toward alcoholism before and after a training program for social caseworkers. *Quar J Studies on Alcohol,* 31:669-683, 1969.
7. Anderson, Dwight: The place of the lay therapist in the treatment of alcoholics. *Quart J Studies on Alcohol,* 5:257-266, 1944.
8. Strachan, J. George: *Alcoholism: Treatable Illness.* Vancouver, Mitchell Press Limited, 1968.
9. Pittman, David J., and Sterne, Muriel W.: The Carousel: Hospitals, Social Agencies, and the Alcoholic. Report presented to the Missouri Division of Health, 1962 (ditto).
10. Belasco, J. A., and Trice, Harrison: Training as a Change, a Constructive Evaluation. *Selected Papers, 17th Annual Proceedings.* North American Association of Alcoholism Programs, Chicago, 1967.
11. Cahalan, Don: *The Problem Drinkers.* San Francisco, Jossey-Bass, Inc., 1970.
12. Driscall, James G.: Community psychiatry. *The National Observer,* 10, No. 32, copyright Dow Jones and Company, Inc., Maryland, August 19, 1971.

CHAPTER V

POLICIES IMPORTANT TO PERSONNEL

J. GEORGE STRACHAN

PART-TIME AND VOLUNTEER STAFF

ACUTE SHORTAGES OF qualified personnel and the urgency of providing services may necessitate the employment of part-time or volunteer staff. However, it is inadvisable to use a disproportionate ratio of either, and never more than sound supervision and staff liaison can sustain efficiently. Supervisory positions and those entailing special responsibilities should be filled by full time staff, ensuring a healthier and sounder personnel structure.

Part-time clinical physicians and consulting psychiatrists may be fitted into medical services. Therapy group leaders, pastoral, vocational and other counselors can regularly perform specific services in which their skills make a worthwhile contribution to total programming. Students can be utilized during in-service training programs in special projects.

Part-time and volunteer staff should have continuous contact with permanent members and be employed for sufficient periods to prevent disruption of programming or personnel. They require direction and thorough orientation to the goals and services of the agency. Their qualifications should be assessed as carefully as those of full time members.

Practical Alcoholism Programming by J. George Strachan, Mitchell Press Limited, Vancouver, B.C. 1971, Part V; Personnel, Chapters 15 and 16.

Volunteer personnel can perform a number of services. AAs and their family members may conduct orientation sessions about AA and Al-Anon. Representatives of other community resources may interpret the services of their agencies. In hospitals, correctional and rehabilitative centers, long-term or former patients can function in therapy programs. Again, all such workers should be screened, understand their specific roles, and be restrained from going off on personal tangents.

REMUNERATION AND BENEFITS

Important to personnel policies are sound remuneration scales and fringe benefits—pension and insurance plans, holiday and sick leave, superannuation. These are essential factors in attracting and holding qualified staff. Since many personnel members are expected to play multiple roles with patients, the professions and the public, over and above normal vocational and avocational interests, remuneration levels should reflect the additional responsibilities entailed.

Effective staff planning should also be concerned with opportunities for professional growth. Professional association and advancement; involvement in community activities; participation in research and other projects; continuing university studies; and where pertinent, lecture or teaching privileges all should also be considered relevant to employment.

Salary structures are a major concern in this field. Ever since inception, the alcoholism field has been plagued by low salaries. They should be compatible with other public health services. Granted that doctorates in alcohol studies have not as yet been devised for alcohologists and that some recovered alcoholics have only the Ph.D. of their experience, remuneration levels should not be a deterring barrier to attracting qualified personnel.

In some regions the health disciplines *per se* are paid less than those of other professions. Clinical psychologists may receive less pay than educational psychologists, perhaps because educators are better organized or receive prior consideration over the needs of mental health. Counselors for institutions and correctional programs are difficult to procure if their levels happen to be based on those of orderlies or guards, who are hardly in the same category of skills.

Workers entering this field may feel that because alcoholic patients require more time and effort and are reputed to be more difficult to treat successfully, work with them may not be very rewarding. This is not so, as trained and experienced workers soon discover. However, if new workers are to learn about alcoholism they will have to be adequately rewarded during the process of their orientation.

Many alcoholism programs, in planning new or expanded services, advertise positions at levels that will not attract the kinds of people needed. A state agency, seeking a new administrative head and additional professional workers, established salary scales which only student graduates could consider. In another program, when qualified and experienced personnel were brought to the attention of a mental health supervisor, he glibly noted, "These people are much too expensive." His whole department suffers drastic shortages of all disciplines with resultant inadequate services. Though countenancing any building expenditure, he frowns upon meeting going rates for personnel. While this is a policy throughout much of the field of public and mental health it tends to be tragically present among alcoholism agencies. Little wonder that offering greater personal compensation, technological interests attract more students and workers, while the humanities suffer.

Qualified workers should be able to transfer internally from one health service to another without serious personal sacrifice. Otherwise, with demands as heavy as they are in some areas of health which pay better, workers won't enter the alcoholism field. Those who do will only use the experience gained as a stepping stone to greener pastures. Is it not time to balance the scales and allocate more of the enormous gross revenues received from the use of alcohol for personnel to combat the suffering it creates?

In General Omar Bradley's words:

We have grasped the mystery of the atom and rejected the Sermon on the Mount. The world has achieved brilliance without wisdom, power without conscience. Ours is a world of nuclear giants and ethical infants. We know more about war than we know about peace, more about killing than we know about living.

STAFF ORIENTATION AND DEVELOPMENT

Agencies with generous budgets may often raid others for staff. Such a practice creates new problems and a serious turnover of personnel in less well endowed agencies. Actually, such raiding may even be carried out on an international basis. One solution open to all is an internal staff development and in-service training program.

It is now acknowledged that since most alcoholics are not penniless derelicts, this spanking new field can be made to pay. Vocationally, it presents an area of service and income for qualified and well motivated workers. However, to entice and hold workers it is imperative that they have the opportunity of being oriented to the field to better apply their skills and experience. Since teaching is not available through normal learning mainstreams, the responsibility for professional growth and advancement must be assumed by alcoholism programs. As vocations in this field attain a respectable status, they must be governed by the same practices demanded in other professions.

This procedure protects workers from being dropped into a treatment or preventive service role without advance training— essential to the reputation of the alcoholism agency and its staff.

In like manner, recovered alcoholics also require practical orientation to the responsibility of their positions. They must be taught to establish positive relationships with other personnel, learn not to confuse personal recovery therapy with that of the agency, and never, because of professional agency relationship, act superior to fellow AAs.

While program staff should receive first and continuing attention, personnel of other resources should have similar opportunities. Oriented, they can then conduct their own courses, providing better service for patients within all facilities. Remember, to inform the personnel of one resource does not reach all workers of every agency; to reach one group of doctors does not enlighten the whole medical profession; to educate one set of teachers does not mean that all students thereafter will be exposed to the same learning process. It is oftentimes a weakness of programming to assume that having provided one round of orientation activities the goals and the technique of education are thereby achieved and fixed into a pattern.

In spite of increasing services at the public level and the phenomenal growth of Alcoholics Anonymous, their combined resources are reaching only a minimal percentage of sufferers. Lacking understanding of the concept of alcoholism as a treatable illness, personnel of other resources have not assumed their share of the patient load. Therefore, before alcoholism services can be integrated throughout the resources of the community, alcoholism agencies must institute and maintain a teaching service. They should provide the personnel to conduct refresher courses, and training seminars. Otherwise, administration is handicapped by uninformed workers within its facilites and among other related resources.

A training course for workers should cover the spectrum of services offered by the agency. Bear in mind that treatment personnel must be aware of the contribution of preventive services, who in turn cannot speak meaningfully about their activities unless treatment oriented. The roles that administration, government, advisory committees and others play must also be understood by personnel. Referral contacts within the community should be defined. These basics must be thoroughly understood by all personnel and not merely by a few supervisors. Refresher training on good manners and attitudes, from the receptionist through the director, are of paramount importance at all times in any community resource. Well informed staff acquit themselves better with patients, the professions, other resources and the public at large.

Personnel, to work with and understand Alcoholics Anonymous, must read their materials, attend their open meetings and expose themselves to the Fellowship. Likewise they must be familiar with the staff and functions of private and public hospitals, hostels, rehabilitation centers, work farms, jail programs, court classes and institutions. How else can they deal intelligently with clients who speak of these other media of help? How can workers talk with knowledge or sincerity about community services or inform professional groups, unless they know something about these activities from first hand contact?

Staff orientation and development does not stop with learning about the illness alcoholism. Personnel should be encouraged to further their training and be given every opportunity to supplement their knowledge and experience. They should participate in studies and investigations; be aided to assume responsibility in their own professional associations; and be stimulated to share their knowledge with their confreres and others.

The agency which encompasses such procedures may seek out and train personnel with sound basic qualifications but who have incomplete formal education. It can guarantee a future for all its members and once solidly established, it need never curb services for lack of staff. Such a program has much less difficulty and conflict between non-alcoholics and recovered alcoholics, or lay and professional members of staff.

Personnel evidencing an interest in switching from one service to another may be encouraged and assisted. If close relationships are maintained with all staff, such interests are known and used to good advantage. Thus qualified personnel is retained rather than lost to another agency. When personnel members share interests, problems and effective procedures, keep abreast of new developments and techniques, cooperatively point to similar goals, programming becomes much more rewarding, *and personnel grows professionally while achieving greater personal satisfaction.*

IN-SERVICE TRAINING

Recently several university students came by to say hello. When the inevitable topic 'where do we go now?' arose, the opportunity presented itself to discuss the needs of the field of alcoholism. A stop for coffee became a full evening session on vocational interests. One lad must soon make a choice between an associate professorship with a period of teaching and his desire to work with problem people. Now twenty-five, he has a B.A. in education and is majoring in sociology. He plans to continue for a doctorate. Though teaching offers more immediate security and advancement, he isn't drawn to this profession but wants to be 'where the action is.' He spent several rewarding summers working with settlement and rehabilitative programs for juveniles.

I raised these questions: "Have you thought about investigating the relationship of alcoholism to delinquency? Have you considered the magnitude and potential of this field of service as your life's work? Do you know anything about it?" These queries got us all going, for this idea was new to them.

Monies are available for investigative studies to encourage student interests. In young adults rest our hopes for effective future accomplishment. For the most part free of prejudice, their potential is boundless. More importantly, their concern with social problems is genuine and deep. The field of alcohol studies offers an opportunity of service for which they can appreciate the need, having seen the ravages of alcohol misuse among their fellow students and peers. What an opportunity is missed when programs do not carry an invitation to students of the healing sciences.

There are also potential workers to be found among students forced, for some reason, to leave their studies in medicine, theology, education or the social sciences. There are also those who, after graduation, do not find the gratification sought in these chosen vocations. Providing that they have sound basic qualifications, many could be retrained to this field.

Participation in meaningful local studies and projects is a sound way to attract new workers. While gathering necessary knowledge the agency is also able to offer its resources to students of all disciplines. Those exposed to the opportunities available may be enticed to *stay put* and work at this service rather than join the *brain drain* to more established fields in other areas.

Similarly, personnel of other agencies can be encouraged to look at this field. Recovered alcoholics desirous of an opportunity to work at the public level can be assessed better while involved with such an in-service program.

TEAM APPROACH

With its many facets—physical, emotional, social and spiritual —the illness of alcoholism demands a team approach to all the disciplines within both treatment and preventive services. While treatment is particularly important to those who are afflicted with the illness, education is the medium by which alcoholics and those close to them are drawn to enquire about and finally to accept treatment. The full recovery of the patient requires the coordinated skills, insight and experience of medical and social sciences, the cooperation of other recovered alcoholics and the good will of society.

Though an overlapping of interests is inevitable, if personnel members operate as a closely knit team there will be no conflict of individual prerogatives. This is evidence of a really competent personnel structure and program. Though the surgeon wields the scalpel, the nurse and anesthetist are vital to the patient's total well being. This principle demands an openminded willingness to learn and work together in accomplishing common goals. This is basic to an effectual approach to comprehensive, resultful programming.

CHAPTER VI

THE PARA-PROFESSIONAL IN A
MEDICAL SETTING

MAXWELL WEISMAN, M.D.

T ODAY'S VAST NETWORK of health care services in the United States is the product of complex evolution. It can be traced back through other lands and distant ages in a tortuous history of simpler systems but ultimately takes root in specialized *healers*.[1] With the multiplication of needs and the finiteness of human capacity in any given situation, assistants and other specialists emerged. The witch doctor may have had to acquire an acolyte and the country doctor, perforce, assign a new role and responsibilities to his wife. Some innovations were spontaneous, almost thrust upon society, and some were the fruits of careful planning. A New York Times article begins, "Plans were announced today for a $900,000.00 program to train men and women, preferably those with some medical experience, to assist physicians in collecting and evaluating a patient's history and physical data . . ."[2]

To the uninitiate, a hospital is a bewildering hierarchy of administrators, attending physicians, surgeons, pathologists, anaesthetists, residents, interns, nurses, aides, orderlies, technicians, dietitions, social workers, psychologists, psychiatrists, students, candy-stripers, pinkies, grey ladies, maintenance workers, etc. etc. . . .[3] Some categories represent on-the-job training or apprenticeships for more lucrative positions but all feed into the optimum delivery of care required to return the sick individual to a healthier life. Some have been selected for more glamorous treatment by novelists and media writers, but the efficiency of the maintenance worker who sterilizes the gloves or the electrician who powers the lights can be as vitally important for life or death as that of the surgeon.[4]

With increasing community pressure on the general hospital to admit patients with alcoholism for the specific purpose of detoxification, old problems arise with new force and thus demand new solutions. The simple repeal of hospital by-laws which may be barring alcoholics from admission under that diagnosis and even the change in attitudes of hospital staffs under the impact of educational efforts by the American Medical Association, the American Hospital Association, the American College of Physicians, the American Medical Society on Alcoholism, the National Council on Alcoholism, Blue Cross and others, are not sufficient to resolve a number of special difficulties.[5, 6, 7, 8, 9, 10]

There is a whole group of chronic illnesses where changes in patients' life style, attitudes and behavior are critically necessary for effective recovery and rehabilitation to take place. Physicians and nurses, with the acute shortages in personnel and increased demands for services, often have no time or training to become involved in education and changing the life patterns of their patients. Diseases like diabetes, emphysema and tuberculosis, cardiac pathologies, arthritis and numerous others, for some considerable time have had their para-professionals, developing for patients special diets, exercises, vocational rehabilitation courses, etc. Alcoholism has been a late-comer. A few medical or semi-medical agencies treating alcoholics were more foreseeing than others and have for years, been employing such personnel (see Chapter IX) but the alcoholism counselor is, today, perhaps the newest of the para-professionals to emerge on the medical scene.

This development in alcoholism is no longer seen as an isolated or sporadic phenomenon. In 1968, Maryland, for example, was the first state after the District of Columbia to pass a Comprehensive Intoxication and Alcoholism Control Law which removed public drunkenness from the criminal system and outlined a treatment and rehabilitation program within the public and private health sector, including detoxification as an integral part of the medical services of a general hospital.* The first annual report of the Maryland Division of Alcoholism Control states:[11]

> More alcoholics than ever before were reached and helped by alcoholism counselors in a variety of locations: in Baltimore, in municipal courts, general and tuberculosis hospitals, housing projects, industry, trade unions, jails, alcoholism and tuberculosis clinics, a special program for alcoholic probationers, a research project, half-way houses, a community mental health center, a settlement house, a ghetto street corner; in the counties, in alcoholism clinics, in industry, in the local health department, in the State tuberculosis and mental hospitals.
>
> More and more effective, alcoholism counselors became available through the federally financed training program operated by the Baltimore City Health Department at its Alcoholism Center. During the year, 24 men and women graduated from six-month courses, all of whom, as students, had been assigned for supervised field work in community agencies.

IN THE HOSPITAL EMERGENCY ROOM

Within the hospital emergency room the alcoholism counselor participates in the management of the acutely intoxicated patient, and under the supervision of the physician or nurse, may be trained to carry out numerous procedures formerly performed by others.[12] He is often better at taking more meaningful personal and family histories, since he can more readily cope with deeply imbedded defenses of denial and rationalization. If he is, himself, a recovered alcoholic, he can more readily identify with the patient in being aware of the psycho-dynamics through his own resistances, projection defenses and substitutive and often symbolic gratifications.

The patient with alcoholism, who is a victim of the mistaken notion that the disease is voluntarily self-inflicted, may feel a great distance between himself and the physician. He may

---

* The Maryland example was quickly followed by Hawaii (1969), North Dakota (1969), Florida (1970), Arkansas (1971), Massachusetts (1971), Minnesota (1971) and a growing list of State legislatures considering similar legislation.

consequently feel closer to the counselor who uses the same language, the same idiom, and has had similar experiences. If he has had difficulty with authority figures he may more readily regard the recovered alcoholic counselor as a self-selected, more dedicated and devoted worker than the professional whom he has traditionally seen as rejecting, cynical and skeptical of his recovery.[13] He may therefore be more honest and open about his difficulties.

Once the physician has cared for the acute medical needs of the alcoholic in the emergency room, if no medical complications exist and there is no danger of the withdrawal syndrome the patient may be discharged fairly quickly to continue his convalescence at home. However, to maintain sobriety, a follow-up program is often essential since the emergency room may become a revolving door facility for the alcoholic who tries to do it on his own. Here the alcoholism counselor may play a vital role in establishing the positive relationship so necessary in motivating the patient to embark on this long-range program. The counselor must reflect three attributes of the staff as a whole: 1) a non-judgmental attitude characterized by a genuine acceptance of the patient as suffering with an addictive illness, 2) a thorough knowledge of the dynamics of alcoholism as a complex, socio-medical illness so that an objective evalution can be made of the patient's needs and capacity for recovery, and 3) knowledge of other agencies involved in follow-up care.[12]

The alcoholism counselor employed on the emergency room staff is usually equipped with knowledge of these resources and often the more helpful agent in effecting the referral. But the real denizen of the revolving door population in both the general hospital and the state and county mental hospital is the homeless and indigent alcoholism patient. As a group, often quickly stereotyped as *hopeless* alcoholics, they have always played havoc with the willingness of the medical profession to be involved in treatment, even detoxification, let alone rehabilitation. A fortuitous development in Maryland, described below, in which the alcoholism counselor plays a key role may well alter that situation, relieve the general hospital of an inappropriate burden and improve existing recovery rates.[14]

IN A QUARTER-WAY HOUSE

For those homeless alcoholic patients who are still too sick to be turned out of the emergency room into the street but not sick enough to be admitted to an expensive hospital bed, the Maryland Division of Alcoholism Control has made possible the establishment of the Quarterway House, an extended care facility for the general hospital. Here such patients following detoxification may stay up to fourteen days and receive not only the medical care prescribed by the hospital physician but also intensive re-education and guidance into a follow-up program for their chronic illness. The alcoholism counselors show films and slides, give lectures, hold group discussions, provide individual counseling, schedule AA and Al-Anon meetings and invite community leaders from a variety of local resources for helping alcoholic persons. A liaison nurse in the general hospital alcoholism services arranges for any necessary return to in-patient hospitalization or out-patient clinics in the event of medical complications and thus provides for continuity of medical care.

The Quarterway House of the University of Maryland Hospital is a twenty bed facility approximately two hundred yards from the emergency room and serves as a model for other general hospitals which have followed a similar pattern. It is staffed entirely by five alcoholism counselors, one of whom is the senior house manager and another the follow-up counselor primarily concerned with the patients' arrangements for subsequent residence, vocational rehabilitation, employment, utilization of social services, etc. The House is used as a teaching facility by the professional schools of medicine, nursing and social work and for rotating duty (7 p.m. to 7 a.m.) by medical students who are paid $5.00 a night.

In the first year of operation, 717 patients were treated at a cost of $14.50 per patient per day, and a total budget of $103,000.00. Although at first the vast majority of patients were indigent, the success of the program in keeping patients sober recommended it as a referral resource to industrial plants with employee alcoholism programs. By the year's end only 50 percent of patients admitted were indigent.[15]

SCREENING OF CANDIDATES

Although training programs to equip alcoholism counselors for work in a medical setting have not yet been standardized, it is abundantly clear that training is highly desirable and rigorous screening of candidates is mandatory. In the case of recovering alcoholics, Twelfth Step work alone is not adequate preparation but should be supplemented by formal training. An extensive period of sobriety is usually indicated, though the length of sobriety to be required before hiring is somewhat arbitrary. Most programs require a two year period although four years would be better. Rare exceptions, however, with only a few months of sobriety have worked out well.

Careful checking of references and personal interviews in depth are essential. The candidate's attitudes must be explored, his ego strength, his ability to cope with such emotions as anger and hostility and his levels of tolerance. It may be useful to structure the interview so that the candidate is actually stressed in the situation in order to gauge his real-life reactions.

The level of formal, academic education is less important than personality and living experiences. He may have only a high school education but should be sufficiently broadminded and flexible not to feel locked into any one treatment modality such as the one which may have been successful in keeping *him* sober. He should be warm and accepting without the need to possess, he should like working with people, be able to establish rapport and empathize.

There is a real need to place female alcoholism counselors in a medical setting. As community attitudes improve and alcoholism is increasingly accepted as a disease, more alcoholic women will emerge from hiding and seek or be brought into treatment. Already the sex ratio in some areas is changing from one to seven to one to four, and may even more closely approach one to one. Valuable experience has been derived from the years of AA activity in which men usually counsel only men and women counsel women. The actively drinking alcoholic woman is usually so unattractive and violates all social standards for women so shockingly, even at low socio-economic levels, that men have serious hang-ups of effectiveness in this area. Likewise, a male counselor may not be able to work with women who frequently defeat or manipulate a man at every turn. Men, too, often focus with women on external difficulties and troubles and cannot, without special training, explore the subtleties of female feelings about being a woman and a female alcoholic. There is, by the very nature of our society, a special loneliness, isolation and inner pain a woman feels and she is often less concerned with flashy, sensational behavior than the male.[16] For these and other reasons relating to the role of woman as a mother figure in general, it is highly desirable to employ women as alcoholism counselors.

PROBLEMS

One of the most serious problems facing the alcoholism counselor working in a medical setting is often his own disappointment. How strange that he should face the possibility of disillusionment with his professional colleagues! This is often the price he must pay for the tangled emotions with which he may embark upon his new career. If he is a recovered alcoholic, particularly one who has achieved his sobriety through AA, he may well have acquired attitudes, all too justified through personal experience that physicians and nurses as a whole, are Johnny-come-latelies in the field of helping sick and dying alcoholics. In his Twelfth Step work he has no doubt encountered many situations in which his sick *pigeons,* needing medical attention, were nevertheless rejected by these *angels of mercy.* How often, in fear for a man's life, had he brought a shaking, sweating, toxic unfortunate to a physician's office or a hospital emergency room only to find the door cruelly shut in his face or, scarcely any better, to be turned out quickly after a dose of paraldehyde or a shot of a tranquilizer? How many consequent deaths had he witnessed?

Then too, how many persons with alcoholism had he heard relate that they *had* been seen by a physician and treated periodically only by the physician's stock-in-trade, a prescription for medication, a month's or more supply of Librium or Doriden or Miltown or a host of other tranquilizers or hypnotics? How many iatrogenic drug addicts had he seen?

In spite of such critical and even hostile feelings, the para-professional also reflects the admiration and regard society accords the physician, the *healer of the sick,* the *arbiter of life-and-death.* He, too, subtly thinks of the physician as little short of God. He is eager to work with this *professional* and often becomes starry-eyed. He may even be somewhat frightened by his own feeling of inadequacy but he *is* eager!

And what does he find? Sometimes a dedicated person, well-trained in his profession yet humble about the gaps in his knowledge of alcoholism and willing to learn from his patients and others. More often, he may find an internist or a psychiatrist who does not wish to work with these very sick people and who is literally frightened by the very patients the para-professional has been dealing with, alone, for many years. In staff meetings he learns that the professional may be more dishonest than the patient and even more neglectful of his responsibilities. He may find a physician who overprescribes drugs and underprescribes himself, who thinks of milieu therapy as busy work and who may be so young and ardent as to be caught up in vital civil rights and social issues, yet somehow, couldn't care less about a forty year old housewife who is drinking excessively.

When the expectations of the para-professional are not met, particularly on a feeling level, he may become hostile and destructive. He may become cynical and generalize his disillusionment. One of the very first considerations in training, then, is to anticipate such conflicts and explore the emotional baggage the trainee carries with him into the medical setting. He should be helped to see the dynamic forces at play behind the surface interactions so that he may be able to function constructively without bitterness. Once at work, a process of communication should exist which makes possible the airing of feelings in a two-way street, since the para-professional may also be regarded as a threat by the professional staff.

The hospital, as the model of a medical setting, is traditionally a hierarchy with a chain of command in which the physician has final responsibility for the patient and his treatment. Orders emanate only from the top and must be sedulously followed to the letter by other institutional personnel. So intrenched, indeed, is this quasi-military structure of hospital health services that community mental health centers also seem to be moving into a hierarchical system of care similar to that of the in-patient model.[17] In this hierarchy each member accepts a defined role and the para-professional working with alcoholic patients may well be assigned a low-man-on-the-totem-pole position.

No organization could be more inimical to the success of a comprehensive alcoholism program than this! The physician must retain his responsibility for the physical, medical and psychiatric treatment of the alcoholic patient while recognizing the value of other aspects of the *total* rehabilitation program which are the responsibility of other individual members of the team, including the para-professional or alcoholism counselor.[18] It becomes important, then, that no distinction in value judgment should be made between any parts of the program. Equal treatment status should be accorded all members of the team, regardless of who the captain is. It can even be argued that the very term *para-professional* should be abandoned if, etymologically, it reinforces the notion of merely being *at the side of* or *almost like* a professional.

Precisely because the alcoholic patient who feels insecure in being accepted, continually tests the helping person and tends to manipulate individuals and agencies in the attempt to continue his drinking, a philosophy of peer relationships is essential. It may even have to incorporate, dialectically, the concept of role diffusion while one carefully defines the specific role differences. Training the staff how not to accede to every patient request to see the doctor requires a knowledge of how to operate to the maximum of one's capabilities while remaining exquisitely aware of one's own limitations as a para-professional or, indeed, a professional. The multidisciplinary enrichment provided by the team does not operate *vis-a-vis* the patient directly then, but through staff discussion and development. This means, of course, that the alcoholism counselor does not act as the doctor but, at the same time, because his salary may be low, is not hired for the so-called menial tasks.

WHEN THE COUNSELOR IS AN AA MEMBER

When the counselor is an AA member he may have to cope with a particular physician's philosophical difference in regard to the use of drugs. He must learn that medication is a legitimate tool of medicine and that it may not only be indicated but can be life-saving. Some AA's are so deeply scarred by the poor medical practices of some physicians that even when they have accepted the temporary value of Antabuse, as they would any crutch, they are frightened by the prolonged use of phenothiazines with schizophenic alcoholics. At the same time, they are themselves learning they can be instrumental in educating the physician to be unmoved by pharmaceutical manufacturers' blandishments.

Another important role conflict must be resolved when the para-professional is an AA member. He will find it difficult to act as a Twelfth Stepper with his own patients in the same manner that a psychiatrist finds it difficult as a therapist to treat his own family members. This does not mean that the para-professional cannot function as an AA member. It simply means that he should function as an AA member outside the medical setting with individuals other than his own patients. He should not sponsor his own patients but introduce other AA sponsors to them.

The work-load is often a problem for the AA member when he is an alcoholism counselor in a medical setting. He may be hired to work from nine to five, but he may have AA meetings night after night. As a result, his social and recreational life becomes inextricably tied to his working day, without any real distinction between them to the detriment of the former. There is no actual change of pace and he soon gets no pleasure or fun out of his life. He may become stale, dull and spiritless. He must quickly learn to set limits for himself, firmly establish himself in one continuous AA program and, wherever possible *not* invite his patients to that group. In rural areas or where only one AA group may exist this is obviously not realistic. Under these circumstances he may introduce the patient to the group and establish another sponsor. He must always bear in mind that he is attending AA for himself and not as a professional worker in the fellowship.

CONCLUSION

So extensive has been the infiltration of alcoholism para-professionals in other care-giving agencies than the traditionally medical ones, that Maryland's experience in coordinating these services for alcoholics may well serve as a model for the comprehensive treatment of other chronic diseases which involve behavioral aspects and whose control has foundered on the mind-body dichotomy.

REFERENCES

1. Buck, Albert A.: *The Growth of Medicine from the Earliest Times to About 1800.* Yale University Press, New Haven, 1917; Camac, C. N. B., *Backgrounds of Medical History,* Paul B. Hoeber, Inc., New York, 1931; Sigerist, Henry E., *A History of Medicine,* Oxford University Press, New York, 1961.
2. *New York Times,* August 20, 1970, p. 20, *First Unit Picked as Doctors Aides.*
3. McGibony, John R.: *Principles of Hospital Administration.* G. P. Putnam's Sons, New York, Second Edition, 1969.
4. Slaughter, Frank E.: *The New Science of Surgery,* Julian Messner, Inc., New York, 1946.
5. Guidelines for admission of alcohol-dependent patients to general hospitals, *JAMA, 210*:121, October 6, 1969.
6. *Admission to the General Hospital of Patients with Alcohol and Other Drug Problems* (approved by the American Hospital Association, September 29-October 2, 1957; revised November 19-20, 1969).
7. Statement on Alcoholism by the Board of Regents of the American College of Physicians.
8. *Physician's Alcohol Newsletter,* American Medical Society on Alcoholism, Inc., 2 Park Avenue, New York, 10016.
9. *Legislation and Public Policy Bulletins,* National Council on Alcoholism, Inc., 2 Park Avenue, New York, 10016.

10. *The Alcoholic American*, National Association of Blue Shield Plans, 1970.

11. *The Year of the Alcoholism Law: Annual Report for 1968 of the Division of Alcoholism Control*, Maryland Department of Mental Hygiene, December 31, 1968.

12. Anderson, R. H., and Weisman, M. N.: The alcoholic in the emergency room, *Maryland St Med J*, July, 1969, *18*.

13. Tuerk, I.: Attitudes and Alcoholics, *Labor Rehabilitation Report*.

14. *Alcoholism Unit Has Halfway House; In-Hospital Treatment, Under the Dome*, Johns Hopkins Medical Institutions, September, 1969.

15. Maters, Wendy: Alcoholism Services, *University of Maryland Hospital Annual Narrative Report, Quarter-Way House* (1970-71, mimeod).

16. Marty Mann answers your questions about drinking and alcoholism, Chapter 8, *The Woman Alcoholic*, Holt, Rinehart and Winston, New York, 1970.

17. Goldston, S. E. (ed.): *Concepts of Community Psychiatry*, Public Health Service, Publication 1319, Washington, D.C., 1963.

18. Davis, Fred T.: *The Para-Professional: An Essential Component in a Multi-Discipline Team Approach to the Treatment of Ghetto Alcoholism*, in selected papers, NAAAP 21st Annual Meeting, September 27-October 2, 1970.

CHAPTER VII

THE PARA-PROFESSIONAL IN THE POVERTY COMMUNITY

RICHARD KITE, PH.D. AND RICHARD KEYES

THE WORKING PREMISE of this chapter is that the para-professional can become a powerful force in the poverty communitys' struggle with alcohol abuse and other human problems. For this premise to become a reality, however, will require a significant shift in the traditional, treatment-oriented approach of professional social and health service agencies which tends to view problems as emanating from the personal makeup of the client. An alternative approach will be outlined in which problems such as poverty and alcoholism are defined within the total context of human interactions with existing institutions, traditions and values, and the role of the social service agent is described as that of a trainer in human problem solving.

Dating from the advent of the Civil Rights Movement, there has been a growing awareness that the professional service giver could not sufficiently understand the problems of the poor, and therefore must be subjected to input from the poor in order to achieve such understanding. From this awareness has emerged the concept of the social service recipient in a participant role. This role has been institutionalized over the past seven or eight years to the extent that consumers are now incorporated as planning task force members, advisory board members, staff members, and in general, everywhere it seems feasible to place a consumer as proof that the agency is forward-looking. One generally positive outgrowth of this concept has been the development of the para-professional role as an approach toward the goal of helping poverty communities help themselves, of enabling the client to solve his own problems.

In reality, however, it seems altogether likely that such approaches are not much different from the traditional one of helping individuals to overcome their own personal short-comings. For it would appear that the basic assumptions of the traditional service agencies have simply been transferred to the para-professional who strives to operate in much the same way the professional has operated, with goals that are similar to those of the professional.

The medical-therapeutic model, which characterizes the traditional approach to social service, is still the prevailing model for training the para-professional. Such training has definite value, but it is certainly limited as a model for training para-professionals. While it may give the para-professional some of the skills required by his agency, it may also destroy the very dimension of his personal experience on which his strength is based, i.e., his identification with the consumer population. To the extent that he is trained to be a therapist and identifies with the professional as a role model, he participates in the myth that his previous experiences resulted from something missing in him and that the professional can provide that missing something; that is, if he has been poor or is a recovering alcoholic, such conditions were a measure of his self-worth, his wholeness as a human being.

One effect of such an identification is to aid the para-professional in the denial of the strengths inherent in his previous experience. He may, for example, become unable to see the tremendous amount of strength that the alcoholic employs to maintain his addiction, or blinded to the skills it required to con a service agency into believing that he has a bad back. These valuable perceptions may be lost to a service agency because of a learning environment in which the para-professional opts to reject his peers in an effort to more closely identify with his newfound role models.

One ultimate result of this process may be to produce an immobilizing effect on the para-professional, for, in spite of his identification with the professional, the fact remains that he is not one. As he is forced to deal with the incongruity between his self-image and others' perception of him, he may choose to resolve this conflict by simply ceasing to perform and retreating into his idealized image of himself.

Thus, if the para-professional is to become a viable component of social service systems, his role will have to be carved out of the very substance and qualities that cause the poverty community to turn to him in the first place, his perceived similarity along dimensions of human experience and understanding. To do so will require a reassessment of the policies and assumptions currently in effect in established social service institutions that select, train and supervise the para-professional, for it is clear that policies which seek to fit the para-professional into existing social service structures, while giving lip service to the concept of para-professionalism, amount to a co-opting of valuable human skills.

That something more than technical skills are required to successfully establish and maintain a helping relationship has long been recognized, but seldom incorporated into systems that prepare persons to help others. Carl Rogers has described some of the characteristics which he has found to be essential in creating a helping relationship, characteristics which center around personal qualities that Rogers associates with psychological maturity. Most of the characteristics Rogers describes fall into three broad categories: 1) awareness of self and behavior congruent with that awareness, 2) an attitude of positive regard and acceptance toward other persons, and 3) non-judgmental empathy toward the feelings and experiences of other persons.

The conceptualization formed by these characteristics has broad similarity to what might be described as a *model* para-professional, one who knows himself, is warm and open toward others, and has feelings for the problems of the people he works with. Although the reference here is to characteristics or qualities of the person himself, it is more appropriate to speak of the processes by which these characteristics are developed in a relationship and furthermore, of the conditions which facilitate these processes. In this context, self-awareness, openness, acceptance and empathy may be construed as goals of the helping relationship in which both parties seek to develop more functional use of their latent inner resources.

The critical issue is to define the broad conditions under which these inherently human skills and resources can be nurtured and mobilized against alcohol abuse and other human problems within poverty communities. In addressing this issue, it is essential to point out that, within the context of the approach being described, the goals of the para-professional and the goals of the poverty community are identical, and that conditions which facilitate the processes by which the para-professional is trained are generally the same as the conditions which enable members of the poverty community to solve their own problems.

The University of California Extension, Santa Cruz, is currently conducting training for para-professional counselors working in poverty community alcoholism programs. The goals of this training program entail the creation of a learning environment in which the trainee actively participates in a variety of learning experiences, analyzes the learning processes through which a specific content area has been covered, and generalizes that learning to other situations and experiences. Specific learning objectives are derived from the application of these processes to the development of skills in dealing with problems that relate to the self, other individuals, groups and families, and entire communities.

The conceptual distinction that is made between the process of learning and the content of learning is an essential characteristic of this learning environment. The particular set of stereotyped expectations that most members of a poverty community bring to a training situation (that learning is the sanctified domain of the intellectual and consists of digesting a massive amount of factual information), must be confronted and dealt with at the outset of training. Of course, this stereotyped view of learning is not confined to the poverty community, but is perhaps more strongly entrenched among the poor because the goals of the traditional educational process constitute a denial of the life style of the poverty community.

One method of dealing with this notion is through the

trainees' participation in direct and continuous experiences which are based on the assumption that all persons have the capacity to learn. For example, the assumption that all persons have the power to learn implies that they are also capable of expressing their learning needs. Thus, the initial learning experience of trainees in our program consists of an assessment of their training needs. Trainees then participate in a planning process to develop a training curriculum based on their expressed needs and the prescribed program requirements.

This latter task serves to directly confront the issue of responsibility for learning and provides the trainee with an opportunity to begin to assume responsibility for his own learning and to control the learning environment. Beginning with issues of self-awareness and personal power, the scope of the trainees' areas of responsibility is gradually expanded to a point at which the trainees as an organized community negotiate with the training staff to assume complete control of the training session. During the second week of training, trainees begin to set the, training agenda for the remainder of the session, select a number of trainees to serve as trainers, and develop a plan for evaluating the training. These activities constitute affirmative, self-determined behavior that is counter to the para-professionals' myth of not having the capacity to control his environment.

Another condition of the learning environment for para-professionals specifies that the identified trainer is not the sole learning resource, and that learning can be pulled from one's own past experience as well as from other learners. This has important implications for the design of group learning experiences and for developing skills of utilizing a wide range of resources for continuing learning outside the structured training environment.

The policies of a traditional educational institution impart the notion that there are right and wrong answers to learning problems by employing a variety of evaluative measures. The conceptualization of learning as a problem-solving process, however, carries the stipulation that the learner must consider several alternative solutions, some of which may be more appropriate for a specific situation than others. The basis for evaluating the learning process is assumed to lie within the learner himself, in the behavioral changes which effect more efficient problem solving. Just as the learner accepts responsibility for initiating the learning process, so also is he responsible for testing that learning and initiating a new learning process.

These are some of the conditions and assumptions which establish a learning environment for para-professionals that is designed to generate a self-determined learning process which, in turn, develops a higher level of skills out of the experiences and resources of the trainee. Upon moving to a higher level of skills, it then becomes the para-professional's task to train others in his community, utilizing the same processes that he has experienced in training. In order to address this task, however, the para-professional must continue to expand and develop his awareness of the total context of the problems that impact the poverty community. He must include the institutional structures and policies that often either inhibit or counteract the achievement of greater problem-solving capacities on an individualized or collective human level.

Most service agencies or programs that operate today in the poverty community lay claim to being in transition from a traditional posture to the adoption of a two-fold approach to social problems which views the clients' problems as part of the community's problems. The actual implementation of such an approach, as opposed to the espousing of rhetoric, requires that certain conditions prevail in the relationship between the agency and members of the community. For example, the community must give sanction to an agency before that agency can rightfully adopt or accept the community's problems and function on its behalf. Also, the conditions of client involvement in the agency's goals and objectives must neither be proscribed in advance by the agency nor geared to viewing the client in a *recipient* role; rather the client must participate from the outset in the definition of his role as a consumer of services. The para-professional who acts as an adjunct of an agency that has not established these conditions must ultimately be viewed as a token representative.

At the program-operations level, the para-professional must

be given sufficient latitude to enable him: 1) to approach his clients from the standpoint of the clients' interests, 2) to involve his clients as learners in their own problem solutions, and 3) to evaluate those solutions in the context of functional behaviors which may or may not reflect the prescribed goals of the agency such as employment or removal from welfare rolls.

Finally, at the interpersonal level the para-professional's role is to serve as trainer and facilitator of his clients' recovery processes by helping them to identify, analyze and generalize their real problem experiences. As the client, whether an individual, family or group, achieves solutions to problems, the para-professional helps the client to expand his self-image to incorporate such achievements, thereby building a framework for a self-determined process of growth and recovery.

REFERENCES

1. Rogers, C. R.: *On Becoming a Person,* Boston, Houghton Mifflin, 1961.

Chapter VIII

NON-ALCOHOLIC VERSUS RECOVERED PERSONNEL

J. George Strachan

THE QUESTION OF who works most effectively in alcoholism programming revolves about the competency of *recovered* versus non-alcoholic personnel. Since agencies reflect attitudes endorsed by administration, personnel policies may range from those employing only recovered alcoholics to programs that employ only non-alcoholic staff, barring recognized recoveries. Ideally a total team approach suggests a complement of both to cope with the galaxy of components involved—physiological, biochemical, psychological, social and spiritual. No single cluster of personnel or avenue of therapy has achieved sufficient success to be acclaimed the sole answer.

Many non-alcoholic professionals who minimize the role of AA resent the implication of incompetence since they see no reason why their skills alone should not suffice. They forget that following generations of ignoring the problem, their members are only beginning to acknowledge a responsibility to the alcoholic, or to appreciate that many of them lack training and experience in dealing effectually with the illness. Some attempt an A to Z analysis of the patient while ignoring the relevant and symptomatic behavior of the alcoholism itself. On the other hand, the Fellowship of Alcoholics Anonymous, which has

Practical Alcoholism Programming by J. George Strachan, Mitchell Press Limited, Vancouver, B.C. 1971, Part V; Personnel, Chapter 15 and 16.

achieved recognition and success by emphasizing alcoholism as the number one issue, readily acknowledges that some alcoholics do need additional specialist care.

An aware physician emphasizes that his care is but the first rung on the patient's ladder of recovery. An aware clergyman acknowledges that effective pastoral counseling must be coordinated with physical and emotional recovery. Experience proves that such understanding professionals, working cooperatively with recovered alcoholics, are more successful.

An institution involved in a demonstration service for alcoholics did not achieve the success anticipated. Every facet of programming was carefully studied to no avail. Finally members of the personnel were evaluated. It was found that antipathy and a serious lack of knowledge about alcoholism prevailed. Lacking clinical training, recovered alcoholic staff were rejected. Thus discriminated against the latter built defensive walls about themselves and countered: "It takes one to understand one." How could the project succeed?

With tact and understanding all personnel could have been fitted into a team approach, using their full capabilities and allowing each to enjoy respected status while achieving programming goals. Recovered alcoholics do play a very meaningful role in programming in either treatment or preventive services.

Though recovered alcoholics have been responsible for developing, and giving administration to agencies of every size and description, those active in public level programs have had a trying history.

While individual members have been in the forefront of those seeking desperately needed services, AA groups have gone so far as to disown them as *professional AAs* for working in alcoholism agencies. There remain a few AAs who fear and resent their loss of control over programming now that others are moving into the field. Naturally such unhealthy attitudes are reciprocated by non-alcoholic workers. Dissenters on both sides fail to recognize or respect the ideologies and contributions others may bring to programming.

The role of recovered alcoholics is further distorted by the second class citizen status to which they are sometimes subjected.

An advertising executive who, after recovery, wrote an excellent manuscript on alcoholism, was asked in all seriousness by a non-alcoholic program administrator, "Who wrote this for you?" He could not believe the man capable of doing so good a job. Why do so many non-alcoholics assume or suspect that all recovered alcoholics have deteriorated? These implications bedevil recovering alcoholic employees for years until their background is overshadowed by their current competence. Perhaps this is the reason some by policy drop all reference to former addiction and recovery.

It has been my experience as an administrator in this field to hear the complaints of both non-alcoholic workers and AAs on these matters. There also seems to be a tendency to expect all AA members, without exception, to practise every principle included in their recovery program. This is unrealistic. Granted, AA also includes members with feet of clay who only make step one and who merely abstain from alcohol. While encouraged to strive for perfection in the recovery of the whole person, none attains that goal. However, how many non-alcoholics even aspire to such goals?

On the other hand, contrary to the belief that recovered alcoholics are too soft on their own kind, the opposite often is true. Once personally past the pain and fear, some close their minds to the misery and suffering of others. Non-alcoholic professional workers find this frustrating.

A few alcoholics fit the old cliche *you can't make a silk purse out of a sow's ear.* Though dry, they remain gross and self-centered. Never achieving sobriety in its true sense, and unable to grow personally, they attempt to reduce everyone else to their own level. However, as with any illness some patients are more sick than others. They project their own problems and resentments on those about them, forgetting the charity and effort once expended on their behalf.

Most recovered alcoholics perform a capable job of re-directing their lives. The quality of their sobriety is reflected in personality changes which see irresponsible and undisciplined patterns reversed completely. Recovery is never wholly measured by the period of abstinence from alcohol. Through sobriety, the learning process is regenerated and the emotional immaturity with which alcoholics are labelled replaced by growth and stability. Recovery of the whole person develops insight and understanding which many non-alcoholics never learn. Gratitude for recovery is behind much of the drive for personal accomplishment and dedication to the cause of others still suffering.

A recovered alcoholic should not be employed because he or she is a good AA member, or to demonstrate good feeling between the agency and the Fellowship. This is contrary to both professional ethics and the Traditions of Alcoholics Anonymous. Nor should the alcoholic employee become immersed in AA politics. It is essential that he should recognize and respect each loyalty.

Recovered alcoholics may be by-passed for positions which many could fill better than some professionals. Too often it is taken for granted that they will donate their time, energies, funds and services. They alone may be expected to take *off hour* duties and troublesome service referrals. This is wholly applicable within Alcoholics Anonymous positions of service—but it does not stand up in public level agencies practice. Serious conflict and resentment on this score can be avoided by according the recovered alcoholic worker the same status as other members of personnel, on the basis of personal merit and performance.

An arrested education or the lack of a degree can be used to retard a recovered alcoholic's acceptance and advancement. He may carry major supervisory responsibilities, a heavy counseling load or play a senior educational role without attaining the same job classification or remuneration as others with lesser capabilities —but having *degrees*.

A study was done on the relative merits of eleven counselors in an alcoholism out-patient clinic. It was found that one counselor had by far the greatest case load and a much more productive record of recoveries than the rest of the staff. A recovered alcoholic, he carried more responsibility than his supervisor. However, his lack of a formal degree precluded the classification and remuneration he merited. Properly evaluated, his capabilities recommended him to the supervisory position. Though having years of sobriety and excellent experience in the social services, with education and training that gave him the equivalent of a master's degree, professional associates refused to countenance his appointment to the position he deserved. He was lured away by a treatment director, who, recognizing his true potential, classified and paid him what he was worth.

Those involved with personnel under the tension of dealing constantly with people's problems, retain no illusions about the perfection of any one individual or group. Recovered alcoholics, in the desperation of their illness, have learned all too bitterly to have no illusions whatsoever for the glamor of a degree in itself.

We tend to forget the human factor in comparing alcoholics with non-alcoholics. Both are people with more similarities than differences. Both are affected by, and react alike to, the same forces and problems in life. Neither is any better or more respectable than the other. As like human beings, they should live and work together as partners and friends with mutual harmony and esteem.

Neither non nor recovered alcoholics, lay or professional, have every requisite to cope with the needs and demands of treatment and preventive services. Recognizing these limitations, can we, at this juncture of time and experience, really establish professional standards for personnel in the field of dependencies and addictions? Do we mean adequately trained, aware, knowledgeable, understanding, experienced and interested workers? If so, they are scarce indeed. With treatment and preventive services as complex as they are; with the rapid advancements currently in effect; with the lack of organized schooling or training in this specialization any key *professional worker* is a layman in more phases of programming than those wherein he is an expert! What further proof is needed of the importance of lay participation in alcoholism programs since this term truly includes those who picture themselves as qualified professionals.

Several of the finest programs in operation: Chit Chat Farms in Robesonea, Penn., The Cumberland Foundation in Nashville, Tenn., The Donwood Foundation in Leaside, Ontario, Guest

Houses at Lake Orion, Mich. and at Rochester, Minn., The Hazelden Foundation in Center City, Minn., and Lynnville in Jordan, Minn.—to name a few—incorporate recovered alcoholics in every phase of their programming to ensure comprehensive care. These facilities are known worldwide for the quality of recovery achieved by their patients.

Other health fields require special job categories and descriptions to meet their unique needs. The very newness and nature of the services entailed in alcoholism programming demand personnel qualifications different from the standards in effect. This is a primary concern in establishing a sound personnel structure.

It is essential, therefore, to fill every post with the person having the best qualifications. Similar principles should prevail for both non-alcoholic and recovered alcoholic applicants. If, incidental to every basic requirement sought, it is also possible to add the experience and dedication of a recovered alcoholic *who has re-achieved stability through recovery* then an added bonus and capacity is brought to that position.

CHAPTER IX

ALCOHOLICS ANONYMOUS MEMBERS AS ALCOHOLISM COUNSELORS

JAMES McINERNEY

W E HAVE TAKEN giant steps forward from those days when alcoholism diagnosis and treatment either did not exist or were pitifully limited. For many years, medicine and para-medicine have not been willing enough to accept the care of alcoholics.

It is generally accepted that AA, as a treatment form, has been most effective in producing and sustaining recoveries. Much of the treatment on the community level has been left to Alcoholics Anonymous. The growth of interest and involvement by medical and para-medical people is of great significance in the treatment of alcoholism.

Concerning this, R. H. Moore, a psychiatrist knowledgeable in alcoholism, makes the following comment:

> A study by Hayman of attitudes toward alcoholism by psychiatrists in Southern California revealed that half reported no recoveries whatsoever, and 80 percent of these with any success reported 10 percent or fewer recoveries. Most advocated some form of psychotherapy despite their pessimism about its value. On the other hand, 99 percent of them approved Alcoholics Anonymous, 77 percent having referred patients to AA. Of the patients they knew in AA, 40 percent had been abstinent up to one year, 20 percent for two years, and 10 percent over two years with about 50 percent *well adjusted*, certainly a much more positive statement than they made for their own work.[1]

In all truth, it must be said that the treatment services in use today are in large measure the outgrowth of the dedication, determination and commitment of alcoholics, most of them members of Alcoholics Anonymous. Together with their loyal friends and supporters among the clergy, and from the fields of medicine, psychiatry, psychology and social work, they have worked unstintingly in the development of effective treatment programs against the disease, alcoholism. A natural by-product of this concern and involvement is the use of recovered alcoholics,* generally A.A. members, as lay therapists or counselors on alcoholism treatment teams throughout North America.

There have been many strong links in the chain of para-professional alcoholism counselors from the pioneer days of Countenay Baylor, the first recognized lay therapist.[2] Baylor devoted the major part of his efforts for four decades from 1912 on to the treatment and reeducation of alcoholics. His protege, Richard Peabody, first treated by Baylor for alcoholism and then trained by him as a therapist, developed and elaborated Baylor's methods in treating alcoholism. A book written by Peabody in 1930, *The Common Sense of Drinking*[3] embodies these methods, and remains to this day a reliable source on treatment techniques for practicing alcoholism counselors. Another successful lay therapist, Francis T. Chambers, a student of Peabody's, played a significant role in gaining acceptance for alcoholism counselors in medical institutions. This was by reason of his close association with the psychiatrist Edward Strecker, M.D., ScD., with whom he worked treating alcoholics in Philadelphia hospitals. Chambers and Strecker co-authored a classic in alcoholism literature entitled, *Alcohol, One Man's Meat,* which went through several printings between the late 1930's and 1950.[4]

It seems that the involvement of recovered alcoholics in AA as full-status members of a treatment team was initiated by a psychiatrist, Nelson J. Bradley, M.D. at Willman State Hospital, Willman, Minnesota, as early as 1950.

––––––––––

* There is controversy over the use of the term *recovered* or *recovering* in describing an alcoholic whose alcoholism has been arrested. Since recovery is regarded by AA members as a continuing process, the AA member counselor is perceived by them as a recovering alcoholic in contrast to his designation by his professional colleagues as a recovered alcoholic.

Today, the place of recovered alcoholic AA members as alcoholism counselors has been well established and defended;[5] counselors are no longer on trial as a group. The work of Marty Mann, Dr. Milton Maxwell of Rutgers[6] and the famous Krystal-Moore *debate* on *Who is Qualified to Treat the Alcoholic?* all attest to this. Many AA members are uniquely qualified to serve as a member of an alcoholism treatment team by reason of the fact that they have made a recovery from the illness. Because they have had to pass through the struggle of becoming their own person, these lay counselors have a deeper appreciation of that struggle as it occurs in others. They bring to their role an excellent model of a recovered alcoholic.

The dimension of having lived the experience also puts the alcoholism counselor in an excellent position to readily recognize the various manifestations of the disease. He can be in touch, both intellectually and emotionally with where the patient is, and can have a sharp awareness of what constitutes reasonable behavior in the hundreds of individuals he has seen work through similar problems. Furthermore, his first hand experience can allow the AA member-alcoholism counselor to get to the rationalization system of the alcoholic quickly, and gives him an awareness of what is realistic time-wise for treatment.

There is overwhelming evidence not only in alcoholism, but in some other health problems, that in the treatment of the condition a high attrition exists. It is skill in the therapist that keeps treatment in motion. Because of his experience with the illness and with AA, the recovered alcoholic can develop an ability to accurately gauge degrees of hostility and resistance to treatment and quickly get to the areas of responsibility and attitude change. The areas are well known to him and he is sensitive to it because of his familiarity with steps 4, 5, 8, and 9 of AAs twelve steps.* The AA member-alcoholism counselor

---

*4. Made a searching and fearless moral inventory of ourselves.
 5. Admitted to God, to ourselves, and to another human being the exact nature of our wrongs.
 8. Made a list of all persons we had harmed and became willing to make amends to them all.
 9. Made direct amends to such people wherever possible, except when to do so would injure them or others.[8]

can sense, too, where attraction ends and building dependence in the alcoholic begins. Likewise, he becomes an accurate judge of whether the formula for the recovery program being used is too rigid on the one hand, or too easy on the other. Finally, the AA member-alcoholism counselor can be in a much better position to handle referrals to AA, Al-Anon, and Alateen than most skilled and trained professionals.

There is a wide range in the status and degree of involvement allotted to alcoholism counselors in treatment centers. In some private and tax supported programs, the use of recovered alcoholics as counselors on treatment staffs is still considered to be out of place. It is the sincere conviction of many otherwise knowledgeable program directors, administrators, and physicians that only a fully qualified physician is in a position to diagnose and treat alcoholism. For many years the Georgian Clinic had no recovered alcoholics on its staff. Dr. Alfred Agrin, physician on that program, believed that, "Within a professionally organized clinic, there is room for none but highly professional people."[9] And this, despite the overwhelming evidence offered by Dr. Robert A. Moore to show the need and benefit of non-psychiatric treatment modalities for alcoholism where AA member-alcoholism counselors would be the therapists of choice. John E. Keller, Administrator of Lutheran General Hospital Rehabilitation Program says it well:

> Therefore, the *team approach* is essential. The professional people need AA, but AA also needs the professionals. AA has become aware of and given expression to this need. *We need to be friends with our friends.* It is regrettable that some AA's and some professionals have the need to go it alone in helping alcoholics to recovery. One of the most interesting, enlightening, and rewarding aspects of the treatment of alcoholism is the inclusion of alcoholics who have recovered within AA as lay *therapists* on the treatment team.[11]

There are treatment programs that give lip service only to the prudence of employing AA member-alcoholism counselors. Prior to the days of greater enlightment this was an appeasement tactic used to keep the AA community happy: this was true particularly in cases where the AA community happened to be a major source of referral for the facility in question.

Today, in most successful and highly regarded treatment centers, the AA member-alcoholism counselor is a vital member of the treatment team. Hazelden, in Minnesota, one of the oldest, largest, and most effective treatment facilities in North America makes the fully developed and well trained alcoholism counselor the central treatment person. In each unit of twenty-two patients an alcoholism counselor serves as leader-coordinator.[12] Aiding him is an assistant and a student counselor. This facility is and has been a training program for alcoholism counselors for many years. Psychologists and social workers on the treatment staff are engaged in research, teaching, consultation, and lecturing to patients. Virtually all the individual counseling and group therapy is in the hands of the alcoholism counselors, as well as most of the lecture work.

It would be unfortunate to create the impression that recovered alcoholics, members of AA, work only in treatment settings. There are hundreds working throughout North America as community alcoholism educators, and guidance and referral counselors in local and regional alcoholism councils. There are probably as many or more working in industrial settings. It seems reasonable that the basic criteria for all of these counselors be quite similar, with the exception of special community training for those persons working in alcoholism councils.

At Lutheran General Hospital Rehabilitation Center in Park Ridge, Illinois, the alcoholism counselor finds himself a team member of equal status and responsibility with the clergyman and the social worker. Patients are referred, at random, to either of the three as primary therapist or counselor. These three backgrounds form the nucleus of each of the three identically composed treatment teams. It is especially noteworthy that academic experience and social-cultural differences distinguishing team members melt away the first year the team works together.

James Lamb Free, another one of the greats in the lay therapist-alcoholism counselor chain reached his prime as a writer and lay counselor in the 1950's and '60's. His book,

Just One More,[13] is a classic in alcoholism literature and has been an instrument in guiding thousands to recovery from alcoholism. Free felt that the need for alcoholism counselors would eventually dwindle as more and more physicians learned to diagnose alcoholism and put the alcoholic on a safe course to recovery. In fact, he was so convinced of this, that he scuttled his private practice as a lay counselor.

What Free anticipated has not yet happened, and, as a matter of fact, the demographic expansion has caused the physician to increasingly meet his responsibility for the care of alcoholics by the involvement of para-professional alcoholism counselors. It is significant that in the last twelve consultations held by Lutheran General Hospital alcoholism programs, every hospital was prepared to include an alcoholism counselor, AA member on its staff. In four of these consultations the alcoholism counselors were brought to the meeting together with the physicians, psychiatrists, social workers, and directors of nurses.

This trend is not limited to the private sector. The recent and current alcoholism programs at the Federal level within the Postal Service and other tax supported programs for depressed communities require the training and employment of alcoholism counselors who are recovered alcoholics. In many instances, these counselors are also members of AA. Several state and provincial alcoholism programs also have the requirement that the alcoholism counselor be a recovered alcoholic. Whether or not AA members are used as alcoholism counselors is, in a large measure, determined by the philosophy and orientation of the alcoholism program directors.

Relatively uncomplicated criteria can be used in the selection of AA members as alcoholism counselors. Both men and women can serve in this capacity, and in either case it is the author's opinion that a minimum of five years of unbroken sobriety should be required. The candidate for the counselor position should likewise be active and respected in his AA community, participating regularly in a recognized group of Alcoholics Anonymous. Alcoholism is a chronic illness, and AA is recognized as the most effective long term therapy for that illness. Consequently, alcoholics should be active in Alcoholics Anonymous. Counselors, as recovered alcoholics, are no exception. Unless a counselor enjoys this kind of relationship with his AA group, he cannot work effectively with patients, since only those AA members who are "working the program" are in a position to expect similar responsibility in the behavior of the counselee.

In addition to the preceding requisites, there are additional personal qualities to be sought in those who would be counselors. First, the recovered alcoholic-counselor should be reasonably at peace with himself and be characterized by a lively faith, an undaunting hope, and a generous love for others. He needs enthusiasm and dedication for the difficult task he is undertaking, and the latter is sometimes a two-edged sword. Furthermore, he must possess qualities of genuineness,[14] honesty, forthrightness, and firmness, which must be tempered by empathy, understanding and fairness. He has to have the ability to relax patients and establish rapport with them, but simultaneously he must be able to work comfortably with professionals in a professional treatment setting.

AA member-alcoholism counselors can work effectively with alcoholics if they know who and what they are. It is established that recovering alcoholics as a group have a low self-image with strong needs for approval. If a counselor always needs to be the good guy in the white hat, he will not be of much service in the treatment program.

Counselors are respected, but not necessarily liked, by most patients in treatment programs. Later, however, when these patients are well on their way to recovery, most indicate their appreciation for the counselors directive technique and firmness, as well as some of the anxiety which he left with them.

Some of the skills essential for alcoholism counselors can be acquired through effective training programs for counselors. Speaking of the need for training of personnel to work with alcoholics, Dr. Robert Moore says:

> . . . we should direct our efforts at training personnel who, though not having complete professional training, can do a reasonable job with awareness of their limitation.[15]

Formal training programs in treatment settings seem the most desirable for accomplishing this. For one thing, through such programs the counselor can acquire expertise in diagnosing alcoholism. Dr. Nelson J. Bradley, chief of psychiatry at Lutheran General Hospital, and medical director of the alcoholism program, makes the following comment concerning this:

> Any alcoholic admitted for detoxification would certainly be seen by an expert in the field to establish the diagnosis of alcoholism. The expert does not necessarily have to be a physician . . .[16]

He goes on to note that recovered alcoholics, active in AA may be used for this purpose. A qualified alcoholism counselor should be able to diagnose alcoholism in no less than a ten minute period with the patient. He should be able to set into motion, immediately, guidance and referral for the alcoholic and for those significant in his life. He should be completely at ease with an alcoholic in any degree of treatment from coma to years of sobriety. As well as formalized training, a special in-service, weekly training program for alcoholism counselors is a must. This program should not have an AA flavor but rather deal with opinions and publications by respected authors in the helping professions.

Through adequate training programs, alcoholism counselors can also acquire skill in determining whether treatment should take the psychiatric or the pragmatic route. He can learn to recognize whether neurotic behavior manifested by patients is primary or secondary, though the determination of this is the responsibility of a psychiatrist. It sometimes takes a few days to get a *dry cortex* in order to know what condition exists. The counselor is often the first one in a position to recognize the symptoms, and from training and experience should be able to check with the psychiatrist who makes the ultimate determination. Unless the alcoholism counselor acquires this degree of expertise his training is deficient.

Effective training programs will be instrumental in developing skill in the use of counseling techniques by alcoholism counselors, as well as in providing experience in both group and family therapy. It is noteworthy that some of the most vigorous and fruitful therapeutic group work has been done by alcoholism counselors who are members of AA and have been trained both in theory and in practice in the methods of group therapy.

Treatment programs that find manpower shortages in all categories of helpers can add AA member-counselors to the list. There are many who would be counselors but who are lacking in both the training and the stamina necessary for the job. There are those who have been only mildly involved in AA during their active years, and feel that counseling would be a nice easy job for retirement years. Such should be reminded that hardworking iron workers and longshoremen are often in better physical, mental and socio-spiritual shape at the end of a work week than are alcoholism counselors.

There seems to be little doubt, especially among reliable AA member-counselors that their roles are complimentary and supplementary to those of other members of a treatment team. Some overlapping of roles occurs which must be understood. For example, in referring a pre-teen son or daughter of an alcoholic for psychiatric treatment, the social worker would generally carry most weight. However, when casework becomes necessary to plan for the future of the alcoholic himself, for a job, housing, or retraining, the alcoholism counselor member of the team might be more influential in the planning process.

Dwight Anderson, realizing as far back as 1944, the usefulness of recovered alcoholics as members of alcoholism treatment teams had this to say:

> They can be made increasingly of use in the future if we learn how to select them, how to train them, and recognizing the scope of their function, learn how to use them in cooperation with the social worker, the psychologist, the physician and the psychiatrist.[17]

It seems that what has already been said about using AA members as alcoholism-counselors might equally apply to Al-Anon members.

There is such a similarity between the ideology of AA and Al-Anon that there is no reason why a well integrated knowledgeable member of Al-Anon would not make an excellent alcoholism counselor. In some counseling situations the Al-Anon member may even be preferable.

Alcoholism counseling, like any other vital, growing field of endeavor, is beset with many sources of potential or actual problems. Some of these derive from the AA member-counselors themselves and others stem from the institutions which sponsor alcoholism programs.

As indicated in the Krystal-Moore *debate*, some alcoholism counselors are attracted to the treatment field in order to handle their own addictive or religious problems, adding complications to the treatment situation.[18]

Still another complication arises when AA member-counselors become involved in the treatment of others without first having resolved their own emotional problems. Of these Krystal says:

> The former problem drinker, however, who controls his drinking on the basis of his AA activities, but who has not discovered and effectively worked through his own emotional problems, is in a worse position to function as an individual therapist to the alcoholic than a person without a history of alcoholism in the past but with no experience.[19]

There are many helpers in the field of alcoholism designated as counselors. When one small child tells another how to make a wagon work, he is counseling. No one has a monopoly on this kind of counseling. Rather, the world is full of counselors. Some of them know whereof they speak; others, not so.

In some of the skid row missions, a person, sober a week, is referred to as a counselor. Some towns, cities, counties, states, provinces, and federal governments have hired as full-time alcoholism-counselors, individuals with little or no sobriety or stability, but with a good degree of political resourcefulness.

Sometimes the agency and the recovered alcoholic show such great urgency about his beginning to work, that adequate screening for knowledge, and suitable emotional fiber and capacity for training are neglected in the selection process. Adherence to criteria for behavior and responsibility in the selection and training of candidates for alcoholism counseling, whether the counseling is to be done on a volunteer basis or for pay, is vitally essential.

In volunteer programs, without financial reward, and often on a part-time basis, it becomes imperative to sort counselors out for dependency, transference, hostility, and other psycho-dynamic problems. Under the guise of counseling there has appeared a great deal of wet nursing and coddling, and AA member-counselors have been as guilty of these as others in the field.

Whether counselors are salaried or not, it is essential that there be criteria for determining whether they are competent. At the present time, that measurement is often predicated on the reputation, real or imaginary, of the institution that trains and/or employs the alcoholism counselors. The same may be said of physicians, psychologists, social workers, clergy and nurses.

The need for standards for judging performance was clearly brought out in the Krystal-Moore discussions in these words:

> We feel that the problem of personnel is so basic that a failure to resolve it precludes effective action in the rehabilitation of alcoholics. Surprisingly, many state governments which sponsor alcoholism programs have failed to set up or even consider the minimum standards necessary for alcoholism clinic personnel. Neglecting to set up requirements for staff training would be un-thinkable in the state's mental health programs.[20]

There is no doubt then about the need for establishing standards for quality performance by AA member alcoholism-counselors. Efforts to bring this about through the establishment of such organizations as the Minnesota Alcoholism Counselors Association, one of the oldest and most impressive, are indeed to be applauded. However, such efforts must proceed with great caution. With standardization comes an exclusiveness, an isola-tion, a power block, a kind of thinking and procedure that militates against an informality that has characterized the coun-selor's worth. Efforts at certification and qualification standards for AA member-alcoholism counselors should be approached slowly and prudently.

While there is a real need for AA members on treatment teams, they have to take care not to use AA affiliation to foster their professional career lest their AA membership suffer. On the other hand, to safeguard their professional career, they must not use it to enhance their AA status. It is also necessary that they stay unencumbered from AA structure above the group level except in rare instances.

There must be sharing and trust in the AA-professional marriage as well as in any other. AA member counselors must understand that non-AA professionals do not have as much manpower to draw on. Also, alcoholism counselors have to recognize that the uniqueness of pure professionals lies in their variety of training and techniques. Both groups must be aware that *attitude* is more important than *technique.*

AA member-counselors need great depths of understanding and emotional commitment to what they have verbalized in singing the praises of AA. We have heard some AA professionals speak apologetically of AA. We have even seen some of them abandon it, although the latter most often proves to be a disaster course.

The real worth that brought the now alcoholism counselor to AA in the first place must not be lost, adulterated or disguised. If he does not believe in what he says about the effectiveness of AA he should quit and sell conventional products in which he can believe.

There is yet another situation which may become a problem area for the AA member-counselor. They know what *easy does it* means, but often find it difficult to practice in a paid job situation. As case loads mount, counselors may have to dilute or even eliminate some services. They may begin to feel guilty because they are spending a diminishing amount of time with their patients. Then, they may fall into the trap of immoderation by trying to maintain a quantity of service that is predicated on the guilt-responsibility factor which they developed in earlier AA associations. They work longer hours, become irritable and neglect home associations. Fellow workers notice that they have fallen victim to production competition. Sometimes this is an insecurity-based competition in which compulsive work begins to substitute for former drinking. This is another form of addiction. To work effectively, counselors have to know their own needs as well as patient and job needs. An illogical truth worth remembering is that, even though the counselor is giving his best, patients often make it despite him and his efforts. He must be prepared to leave something to God.

An additional problem source stems from the fact that some AA member-alcoholism counselors tend to discredit the efforts of their non-alcoholic counterparts. This is because AA members have an added dimension which others lack; they have experienced alcoholism. AA member-alcoholism counselors may sometimes even be more familiar with the alcoholism literature. This can lead to impatience with the *naivety and prejudice* of non-alcoholic counselors. At this point, alcoholism counselors must ask themselves what they have to offer. Is it counsel to patients only? Not at all! They must begin to share their experience, knowledge and skills with others while continuing to multiply their own skills.

Many pure professionals, like early AA members, are not too teachable in the beginning. Sometimes it is necessary to give the ink on the credentials time to dry. This may take two years if the professional is exceptionally acute, but about 24 months if he is not quite so sharp. AA hybrid professionals need just about the same amount of time to lose their absolutism, to really believe they are in the *big league,* to recognize that there is a difference between bread and butter counseling and 12th step work and finally, to determine whether or not they are suited for the work. On the other hand, if the counselor finds that he is continually defending his counseling status to an inordinate number of die-hards in the AA community, he should take a second look at himself, because die-hards are few in number today.

The term AA Counselor has been called a misnomer by the General Service Conference of Alcoholics Anonymous.[21] In an article in the *Grapevine,* John Norris, non-alcoholic Chairman of the General Service Board, refers to *AA Counselors* in quotes.[22] Despite the rationale and clear explanation at the very top level of AA that there is no such terminology as *AA Counselor,* there is a persistency on the part of individual members of AA and others working within alcoholism to refer to alcoholism counselors, member of AA as *AA Counselors.* This may seem to be a small enough point, but as long as this confusion exists, there will continue to be an impaired relationship between these counselors and those with whom they work.

In summary, it might seem from the substance of this chapter that the writer would build from AA member alcoholism-counselors another elite corps of experts who would develop their own language, make their own rules, and end up being another helping *island*. In part, this is true, but in another sense it is not so. An alcoholism counselor should be a knowledgeable expert, an expert in knowing what should be done in treating alcoholics, and an expert in knowing how to do it. However, he must also work with deep awareness that he is only one part of a team whose coordinated efforts are necessary if alcoholics are to be restored to health physically, mentally, socially and spiritually.

REFERENCES

1. Moore, R. H.: Who is qualified to treat the alcoholic? III, Advantage of nonpsychotherapist, *Quar J Studies on Alcohol,* 24:712-718, 1963.
2. Anderson, Dwight: *The Other Side of the Bottle,* A.A. Wyn, Inc.: New York, 1951.
3. Peabody, Richard R.: *The Common Sense of Drinking,* Little, Brown & Co.: Boston, 1930.
4. Strecker, Edward, and Chambers, Francis T., Jr.: *Alcohol, One Man's Meat,* MacMillan Co., New York, 1949.
5. *Alcoholics Anonymous Comes of Age,* Alcoholics Anonymous Publishing Co., Inc.: New York, 1957, p. 117.
6. McInerney, James: The use of alcoholics anonymous in a general hospital alcoholism treatment program. *Medical Ecology and Clinical Research,* 3:22, No. 1, 1970.
7. Krystal, H., and Moore, R. H.: *loc. cit.*
8. *Alcoholics Anonymous,* Works Publishing Co., Inc., New York, c. 1939, 1947, p. 71.
9. Agrin, A.: Comment on Krystal-Moore Discussion 'Who Is Qualified to Treat the Alcoholic?' *Quar J Studies on Alcohol,* 25:347-349,
10. Moore, R. H.: *loc. cit.*
11. Keller, John E.: *Ministering to Alcoholics,* Augsburg Press, Minn., Minn., 1966.

12. Anderson, Daniel: Who is an Alcoholism Therapist? Paper presented, N.A.A.A.P. Annual Meeting, Bismark, N.D., 1962.
13. Free, James L.: *Just One More,* Coward-McCann, Inc.: New York, 1955.
14. Truax, C. B., and Carkhuff, R. R.: *Toward Effective Counseling and Psycho Therapy,* Aldine Publishing Co.: Chicago, 1967.
15. Moore, R. H.: *loc. cit.*
16. Bradley, Nelson A., M.D.: Alcoholism is a treatable disease, *Medical Ecology and Clinical Research,* 3:3-6, 1970.
17. Anderson, Dwight: The place of the lay therapist in the treatment of alcoholics, *Quarterly Journal of Studies on Alcohol,* 5:257-266, 1944.
18. Moore, R. H.: *loc. cit.*
19. *Ibid.*
20. *Ibid.*
21. *General Service Final Report of Alcoholics Anonymous,* New York, 1970. pp. 18-19.
22. Norris, John M., M.D.: The Hazards of A.A.'s Counseling for Pay, *A.A. Grapevine,* October, 1970.

CHAPTER X

UNDERSTANDING AND RELATING TO ALCOHOLICS ANONYMOUS

MILTON MAXWELL, PH.D.

E VEN THOUGH MUTUAL regard between Alcoholics Anonymous and members of the helping professions has been increasing in recent years, certain strains and stresses remain. Most of them have been described by the writer.[1] But, central to all the difficulties, whether as cause or effect or both, is a lack of knowledge, each about the other. Except for detoxification, many members of AA have little awareness of what the various professionals have to offer. Conversely, many non-alcoholics have little acquaintance with AA and little understanding of what really happens in AA and what its therapeutic dynamics are like.

Whatever the lacks, these uninformed pictures lead quite logically to dim views of each other's therapeutic capacities, especially with regard to the personal and interpersonal reorientation and relearning which are basic to recovery from alcoholism.

Each set of views has a natural history,[1] so there is no point in blaming anyone. But neither is it necessary to perpetuate the variety of unfortunate stereotypes still being held. In fact, in view of the enormous unmet need, with 90 per cent or so of alcoholics never receiving recovery help, the continuation of stereotypes which bar or hinder cooperation and mutual appreciation becomes intolerable.

It must be emphasized that this is a two-way street. But, as the title indicates, this chapter is to be about AA. Furthermore, because *relating* to AA depends fundamentally upon *knowing* and *understanding* AA, the focus of this short chapter will be upon the latter.

It is addressed to non-alcoholics, whether professional or para-professional, whose responsibilities include contacts with alcoholics; who may have some difficulty in understanding aspects of AA or who would like to know more about AA or who wonder how they might utilize and work with AA in a more productive way.

But first, it should be stressed that one set of barriers to understanding AA has nothing to do with AA *per se*, but rather with *alcoholism* itself. This may be the inability of many non-alcoholic helpers to be accepting enough of an alcoholic to establish a therapeutic relationship with him. Or, it may be an etiological perspective which is not sufficiently multicausal, not giving balanced weight to physiological, psychological and socio-cultural factors which does not give sufficient importance to the process of *learning to drink* in ways which lead to compulsive drinking, and to the power and persistence of this learning; and which is not sufficiently aware of the *complex feedback effects* of heavy and compulsive drinking upon physiological, psychological and social functioning. Alcoholism is *not merely a symptom of a deep underlying disorder,* but is to be seen as an overlay of developments which in effect constitutes a complex, new, condition which must be dealt with in its own right, no matter what else may be needed in a particular alcoholic's case. The more complete a non-alcoholic's understanding of the complex nature and multiple causes of alcoholism, the easier it is for him to understand the multi-faceted dynamics of AA. Obviously, the same can be said about AA members' understanding of what professionals and professionally-directed programs can contribute to the recovery of alcoholics.

As a corollary, the non-alcoholic will also find it easier to understand AA and what it has to offer if he can become fully aware of the alcoholic's dilemma and the range of his recovery needs.

Jellinek's forty-three symptom *Phase Pattern*[2] can be helpful at this point. Even though not all of the symptoms or behaviors occur in a given case, or occur in this order, and even though many alcoholics today move toward recovery at earlier stages, the phase pattern still provides a useful baseline. It offers a description of the alcoholic's progression into a greater dependency upon alcohol, into more difficulties resulting from drinking, and into a mounting struggle to maintain his social and economic footing. Anxieties and guilt feelings pile up, rationalizations are developed, emotional isolation from other people grows. There are physical consequences as well which in turn increase the anxieties, the dependency, etc. Alcohol no longer *works* like it once did, yet he feels impelled to keep trying to make it work. It is all a vicious circle which moves the alcoholic more and more rapidly into a situation where he becomes locked-in, emotionally encapsulated, and unable to break out. He is fearful of what is happening to him, but he is even more fearful of giving up the drinking which was once such a wonderful asset and still functions as a *medicine*. So he keeps chasing the illusory goal of controlled, nondamaging drinking, meanwhile, propping up his sagging ego with rationalizations to the point of an almost impenetrable system.

What can enable him to break out of this trap and take his first steps toward recovery? For one thing, according to this writer's analysis,[3] he needs to become completely disillusioned with his drinking, and this includes utter disenthrallment with his ability to *control* his drinking. But this penetration of his rationalization system is not apt to occur unless certain powerful fears are simultaneously overcome, at least to some degree: 1) fear that he cannot quit drinking, and 2) the even greater fear that without alcohol he cannot possibly live in any satisfactory or even tolerable manner, or perhaps even live at all.

The baffling *lack of motivation* becomes understandable only when the strength of these fears is understood. Without the introduction of *hope* that there *is* a way out of the tragic dilemma and that a satisfactory life without alcohol *is* possible, movement into a recovery program can be cancelled completely by such fears.

With this understanding, we can appreciate the edge which

a para-professional who is a member of AA generally has over the non-alcoholic in introducing hope effectively. The abstract hearsay knowledge that AA will work is not nearly as convincing as the flesh and blood example of the AA member for whom it has. When, in the usual initial contact, the still skeptical prospect observes that the AA member, who is talking to him and telling his own story, has not only succeeded in staying away from alcohol but is also happy, it usually gets through to him. Hope is aroused and his fears begin to melt. Not all at once, obviously. As he attends meetings and sees others who are enjoying this new way of life, the hope grows and displaces the fears more and more. As two AA members put it:

> I had a few alcoholic cures and the last bout I was on was pretty drastic. . . . I figured AA was the only thing left; and it was the example set by a few of my friends in AA that made me realize it had something.
>
> Life in general was futile. I was a periodic drinker and between binges I was ever worried about when the next drunk would start. I was afraid all the time and yet could not explain my fear. At an open AA meeting I saw hundreds of ex-drinkers who were serene. That was what I wanted, and if they could achieve it, I hoped I could too.

It is strategically important that the helper be aware of these two prerequisites for beginning a recovery program, because he often is in a position to help the alcoholic to admit and accept complete disillusionment and, at the same time, to provide hope in a convincing manner. This is a big order, but an understanding, accepting and experienced helper can often make the difference. *Throwing in the sponge* is a little easier to do when one feels accepted and understood and when there is some hope. More non-alcoholic professionals are learning to provide this key assistance, but it is not difficult to recognize the advantage which the para-professional who is a member of AA has. He's been through it. He knows the intense fears, the despair, all the rationalizations. He can identify and the prospect finds it easy to identify with him. Other things being equal, he has a unique leverage.

Once the alcoholic quits trying to manage by himself and

moves into a recovery program, half the battle is won. But the battle can still be lost unless a great variety of additional needs are met. To clarify matters, it is useful to think of recovery in terms of both short-term and long-term needs.

Any recovery program which has a high success rate will address itself first of all to the alcoholic's immediate and short-term needs. What are they? He requires detoxification and the management of his acute physical needs. He needs help in staying away from alcohol, help against yielding to the powerful compulsion to use alcohol to manage his physical symptoms or any other felt needs. He requires *education* about his condition, i.e., the necessity of not drinking at all, the phoniness and slipperiness of his rationalizations. Such education is critically important. The alcoholic also needs a substantial reduction of his *acute* fears and anxieties. He is in need of acceptance, understanding, and a chance to air his guilts and talk about his feelings. He requires additional and repeated reinforcement of his initial hope that his compulsion will recede and eventually lose its power, and that he *can* make the changes leading to a normal, constructive life. He needs to be given a plan of action, a program to follow, a person or persons to relate to as he begins to find his way back to people and to himself.

How does AA meet these short-term needs? Generally today, when facilities are available, the medical profession is called upon for detoxification and the management of acute physical needs. But in less severe cases, or where no detoxification facilities are available, members of AA themselves will surround the prospect with personal contacts, however much is needed. He is talked to, sat with, sometimes taken into an AA member's home for a few days, taken to meetings as soon as possible, and just generously supplied with an impressive degree and amount of care.

So it is, also, with the other short-term needs. AA meets them through personal relationships and the sharing of experience. Through individual members of AA who work closely with the new member, through the several kinds of group meetings, through listening to and identifying with sponsors and speakers, by being accepted and listened to, by being given the twelve-step program of recovery, by rather quickly accepting belongingness in the group, his short-term needs are met and the new AA member finds himself started on the road to recovery. Obviously, not all prospects respond, nor do all prospects receive the optimum amount and quality of personal care and contact. This is especially true in metropolitan areas where the new person may not be pulled into the close relationships which are so basic to AA's overall program of recovery.

In addition to the short-term needs which may be met within a month or several months after drinking has been stopped, the recovering alcoholic requires long-term help which is to be seen in terms of *years*.

He requires continual reminders of his condition, continued protection against *slipping* into his old thinking and his habitual resort to drinking, especially when things go wrong, or in the kinds of low moments which almost anyone has. He needs further physical rebuilding. Even more important, he needs further personality rebuilding: a continuing reduction of his fears, anxieties, conflicts and other emotional liabilities through changes in outlook, attitudes, values and interpersonal perceptions and interactions. In a very literal sense, he needs to *learn* a new way of life, not only outwardly, but in terms of his inner dynamics. All of this constitutes a process of change and growth over time; and it needs a favorable environment, one which provides continuing incentive and reinforcement. The power of the old learning, the old ways of thinking and feeling should never be underestimated, nor should a helper fail to appreciate what a difficult and all-encompassing change all this adds up to.

These long-term needs are also dealt with by the AA program. AA therefore constitutes a most important resource for professionally-directed treatment programs which, while usually strong in meeting short-term needs, are not often in a position to provide for this important range of long-term needs. Obviously, many members of AA could additionally use professional psychotherapy to assist in this growth. Some do now and more will as mutual understanding grows. This should not obscure the fact that the

AA program addresses itself to *all* of the long-term needs and does so in an unusually powerful group setting.

The more the professional helper is aware of the entire spectrum of both short-term and long-term needs, the more effective he himself will be in treating alcoholics. The more he will also appreciate the value of having one or more emotionally mature AA members on the treatment team. Certainly, such awareness will help him to appreciate the value of getting his patients or clients into AA, and helping them succeed in doing so (see Chapter XII by Kent), thus taking advantage of all that AA offers for the extended process of learning the new way of life.

Perhaps some selected quotations from AA members themselves, describing what they had gained from their AA contacts, will illuminate what we have been trying to say.

Originally, some feeling that I was not alone.

The feeling that someone really cares . . . has an interest in you.

Reassurance by seeing and knowing that others are also getting help . . .

A feeling of freedom and trust and relief from anxiety in the company of other honest people.

A feeling of belonging again to the human race, a feeling of strength to try to get back to people again; that was the first time to believe that I could do it.

An education in alcoholism, which strengthens my desire to quit.

I get a very good cross-section of what alcohol has done to others. And knowing how it nearly cost me all that I hold dear, I am more determined to stay on the program as I am very much aware that alcohol and I must not mix *at all*.

A continuous course in psychology and mental hygiene. A closeness of friendship with individuals whom I feel I know deeply and well . . . a deepening of one's love for his fellowman, of one's understanding of the other's problems.

I get very much more out of the meetings large or small, than I have out of anything else for years; I think it is because of the fellowship, the understanding and loyalty that every member of the group shows you.

Sobriety first, but in later years a new way of life.

From almost every meeting some new thoughts, suggestions or ideas which help to interpret and live the program. An indescribable feeling of self-respect, self-confidence or sense of inner well-being.

Education, example, friendship, understanding . . . an interest in the other fellow's problems with the consequent escape from the old alcoholic egocentricity, . . . Here we get our first lessons in tolerance, charity, and humility. Here we learn the very road to sober, sane, happy living.

A sense of being in touch with some power of which I heretofore felt shut off. A sense of well being and worthiness.

Obviously, it takes more than a short chapter to convey what AA has to offer. The writer has described and interpreted AA at some length.[4] He has also listed the substantial changes toward emotional maturity which members of AA have reported.[5] Certain of the AA publications are particularly helpful in giving the outsider an inside view of AA.[6, 7] Such reading can be of great help but it cannot provide a fully adequate substitute for personally attending a number of AA meetings, and of talking in some depth with a number of AA members who are solidly on the program.

Only by such intimate acquaintance can one get beyond the surface aspects to AA's essential qualities—to the reality of the deep emotional and spiritual reorientation—and to the unique socializing power of the AA group. There is more than meets the eye. In fact, the most important dynamics cannot be observed in the open meetings, but rather in the closed meetings and in the still more intimate interactions in small groups before, after, and between meetings. Yet, the more the non-alcoholic helper can learn about AA, the greater will be his appreciation of AA's multiple strengths; and the greater will be his capacity to relate to members of AA and optimally utilize AA in the recovery of the alcoholics for whom he has some responsibility.

REFERENCES

1. Maxwell, M. A.: An Exploratory Study: Alcoholics Anonymous and Professional Relations. *Selected Papers Presented at the Fifteenth Annual Meeting,* pp. 115-130, North American Association of Alcohol Programs, Washington, D.C., 1964.
2. Jellinek, E. M.: The Phases of Alcohol Addiction. World Health Organization. Technical Report Series, No. 48, Aug., 1952. Also in

Quarterly Journal of Studies on Alcohol, No. 13: pp. 673-684, 1952; and in Pittman, D. J., and Snyder, C. R., eds.: *Society, Culture and Drinking Patterns,* New York, Wiley, pp. 356-368, 1962.

3. Maxwell, M. A.: Factors affecting an alcoholic's willingness to seek help. *Northwest Science, 28*:116-123, 1954.

4. Maxwell, M. A.: Alcoholics Anonymous: An Interpretation. In Pittman, D. J., and Snyder, C. R., eds.: *Society, Culture and Drinking Patterns,* pp. 577-585. New York, Wiley, 1962. Also in Pittman, D. J., ed.: *Alcoholism,* New York, Harper & Row, pp. 211-222, 1967.

5. Maxwell, M. A.: Interpersonal factors in the genesis and treatment of alcohol addiction. *Social Forces, 29*:443-448, 1951.

6. *Twelve Steps and Twelve Traditions.* New York, Alcoholics Anonymous World Services, Inc., 1952.

7. *Alcoholics Anonymous Comes of Age.* New York, Alcoholics Anonymous World Services, Inc., 1957.

CHAPTER XI

FOR THOSE WHO WEAR TWO HATS
ALCOHOLICS ANONYMOUS GUIDELINES

PUBLIC INFORMATION COMMITTEE, ALCOHOLICS ANONYMOUS,
GENERAL SERVICE OFFICE

TO BEGIN WITH, DON'T PICK UP THAT FIRST DRINK!

T HAT QUOTATION IS the basic message of the Guidelines, as one AA who *wears two hats* has wisely pointed out.

So this material is limited strictly to suggestions about life as an AA member. *As AAs we do not presume to give advice about professional matters.*

As you will see, the strength and hope shared here stress the value of a strong AA foundation of recovery for AA members who take a job in the field of alcoholism. Hopefully, they will help sustain and enhance such a recovery. *There is nothing here about how to do your professional work.*

In addition, the experience passed on here—based on trial and error efforts over the years—may help our Fellowship maintain the favorable position it now occupies in many alcoholism circles.

FOR WHOM ARE THESE GUIDELINES, SPECIFICALLY?

This material has been compiled for the AA who is a professional in a national million-dollar alcoholism program, as well as for the member who earns his board and room working at a half-way house.

By permission of Alcoholics Anonymous General Service Board.

These are suggestions for the benefit of *any* AA who wears two hats—that is, members who are employed as professionals or para-professionals in alcoholism programs or agencies. This includes people in three types of non-AA jobs in the alcoholism world: 1) *direct face-to-face services to alcoholics* (such as those given by social workers, counselors, nurses, physicians, etc.); 2) program, administrative, research, planning and educational *positions not necessarily involving actual person-to-person services* to alcoholics, and those concerned more with alcohol*ism* than with alcohol*ics*; and 3) *combinations* of the above.

ON WHAT EXPERIENCE ARE THESE GUIDELINES BASED?

These suggestions are based squarely on the actual in-the-field experience of scores of such AA members who took the time to write out their experiences for this sharing-session-in-print. They answered in detail a questionnaire G.S.O. sent them.

In total, their experience amounts to well over six hundred years of continuous AA sobriety and more than four hundred years of professional success. Their positions range from recent casework on Skid Row to heading national programs for many years.

Separate Guidelines on AA Cooperation With Alcoholism Agencies and Facilities are available for AAs who, as individuals, on a volunteer basis, cooperate with such programs and institutions . . . as 12th Step contacts, or as board, commission, or committee members, volunteer orderlies or aides, research assistants, etc.

WHAT KINDS OF AA EXPERIENCE CAN BE HELPFUL IN AN ALCOHOLISM JOB?

1. Several years of good uninterrupted AA sobriety should be behind you before you tackle any paid alcoholism job, AAs who answered our questionnaire agreed. Five years was mentioned most frequently, but a couple of people said three.

"It's just like I tell my pigeons—don't make any big decisions or changes until you have a lot of solid AA recovery under your belt," one man explained.

2. You should have had experience in several groups, not just one, respondents indicated. Besides group jobs, the kinds of AA service experience recommended are: volunteer work in institutions and at AA Central or Intergroup offices, and terms as G.S.R., intergroup delegate or member of some AA committee.

3. Faith, courage, and self-discipline were repeatedly emphasized as attributes an AA needs on *any* job. "And if you don't have them, you'll also learn humility, patience, tolerance, and good humor to survive in the alcoholism business," one member added.

"Remember," wrote another, "*you* may be the only AA experience your non-AA colleagues ever have, so you have to be a wonderful example of what AA can do."

4. Detailed understanding of AA traditions, and how they developed out of experience, is *absolutely indispensable.*

"I read the books ALCOHOLICS ANONYMOUS, TWELVE STEPS AND TWELVE TRADITIONS, and AA COMES OF AGE over and over," one man wrote.

Traditions mentioned often include No. 3—membership requirement; No. 5—primary purpose; No. 6—outside enterprises; No. 7—self-suport; No. 10—non-endorsement; and No. 11—public relations.

5. Up-to-date familiarity with developments in AA was recommended by many, *so you won't misrepresent AA by mistake or through ignorance,* as one member put it. Mentioned as useful for this purpose were *all* AA pamphlets, Guidelines, the Grapevine, *Box 4-5-9,* and the annual (confidential) published *Report of the General Service Conference.*

Others found helpful include *The AA Service Manual, Cooperation but Not Affiliation,* AA Public Information Manual, the *Beginners' Meeting* kit, *Student's Guide to AA, Alcoholism is a Management Problem,* the new *Twelve Traditions—Illustrated* pamphlet, *AA in Your Community,* and *We Want to Work With You*—new pamphlet for non-AA professionals in the field from the G.S. Board's new Professional Relations Committee.

6. In the public mind, AA is often confused with other

organizations in the alcoholism field. So several respondents said it is a *must* to have some knowledge of these agencies and what they do, and how they are different from AA:

> Al-Anon Family Groups and Alateen
> P.O. Box 182, Madison Square Station
> New York, New York 10010

> National Council on Alcoholism
> 2 Park Avenue
> New York, New York 10016

> National Institute on Alcohol Abuse and Alcoholism
> Department of Health, Education and Welfare
> Rockville, Maryland 20852

> Alcohol and Drug Abuse Programs of America
> 1130 - 17th Street, N.W.
> Washington, D.C. 20036

7. Intimate familiarity with AA in the area in which you work, not only many AA groups, but also intergroup offices, committees, clubhouses, etc.—is needed on many jobs.

8. AA contributors to these Guidelines overwhelmingly agreed that it is *professional* skill and experience, not AA membership, which qualifies one for *professional* positions. Several said that continuing professional education and work have also enriched their AA life.

WHAT IS THE BIGGEST PROBLEM IN YOUR AA LIFE WHEN YOU BECOME A PAID ALCOHOLISM WORKER?

At first, and perhaps surprisingly, this may turn out to be other AA members' misunderstanding about your new job.

In AA's earlier days, some of our longer sober members reported they were accused of *making money out of AA*. It was hard not to get a resentment over this kind of criticism.

AA has grown up a lot since then. Even so, our respondents warned that an AA in a new alcoholism job may still be a victim of misinformation or ignorance on the part of other AAs.

This is particularly tricky since you may feel you are being unjustly attacked or rejected. It is tempting to retaliate, get angry at AA, want to *set matters straight,* or *have it out,* which may only make matters worse.

What to do about it: "First, feel quite secure in your own heart and mind," one respondent said, "that your job is a *good* thing and that you deserve getting paid for it—*as long as you do not take advantage of AA for personal gain of any sort, or exploit AA to get your job done.*"

From another: "Don't act hastily. Take time to think it through and discuss it, considering the long-term effects not only on yourself, but also on other people."

Another: "Often, *what seems at first to be a GOOD thing to do quickly in your personal instance may turn out to be, on reflection, NOT the BEST thing in the long run—for yourself, your employing agency, or the Fellowship of AA as a whole.*"

Another: "You are *not* paid to stay sober, to go to AA meetings, to do the 1st, 3rd, 10th, 12th or any other Steps, or to live within the spirit of AA's Traditions. If you do those things on your own, for your own sake, with no pay for doing them, you are *not* a *paid* or *professional* AA member. You are paid for your professional services, not for your AA membership."

But this is not always clear, especially to newer AA members, who sometimes *seem to feel that anyone being paid for doing anything in the field of alcoholism is somehow betraying or compromising AA,* in one member's words.

As AA members become better informed, they realize that many agencies perform for alcoholics services which AA does *not* provide. And *upon reflection, the more mature members realize that for professional services a professional fee is appropriate,* someone else wrote. (Also see pp. 115-117 in AA COMES OF AGE.)

Another respondent said that before taking such a job she discussed it thoroughly with her AA friends to make sure they understood. Several said that keeping in close touch with other AAs who have such jobs does much to ease the hurt, gives you tips for handling such problems, and provides helpful encouragement and support.

In one state, AAs in alcoholism jobs meet twice a year for

an informal week-end of sharing, and say it is a wonderful experience.

"Don't let criticism bother you," an old-timer wrote. Just plug ahead doing a good honest job, and keep on being a good AA member on your own time. The static will pass eventually."

WHAT IS THE SECRET OF SUCCESS, IF ANY, IN WEARING TWO HATS?

Another challenging aspect of wearing two hats is *being sure at any given moment which hat you are wearing*.

Can you keep it perfectly clear *in your own mind* whether you are acting *right now* in your paid (non-AA) job role, or functioning as an AA member?

"Standing at the hospital bedside of an unconscious alcoholic," one physician explained, "there's no doubt it's my service as a doctor that is called for—not some 12th Step talk."

But it is not always that easy to see immediately the right or wrong of some cases.

One medical social worker wrote, "Talking to clients with alcohol problems, I have to think it through very carefully, and consider the possible results, whether to blurt out impulsively my own AA story, or cool it and use my influence as a professional caseworker.

"Two questions I ask myself are (1) what does this patient need most at this minute? and (2) in either case, am I boosting my own ego or putting the patient's welfare first?"

An AA who is an alcoholism counselor in a hospital wrote: "It's not enough to keep it clear in your own head which cap you have on."

"In case conferences about patients, I discovered, painfully, that the *civilians* on the staff, all of whom know I am in AA, got terribly mixed up about AA, because they could not tell when I was speaking as an AA member and when I was playing my impersonal, professional part."

Many two-hatters agreed it is important to explain or symbolize in some way, whenever possible, exactly in which role or context you are behaving.

Here at G.S.O. we sometimes get letters from AAs complaining about the activities of an AA doing a professional job. And we hear from professionals telling us of trouble caused by an AA who neglects his professional duty in order to perform AA functions. Hard feelings on both sides are the result.

Sticking to one role at a time, and clearly demonstrating the difference between your AA actions and your job performance, is plainly in the best interests of *both* the professionals and AA.

WHAT ARE SOME METHODS USED TO KEEP ROLES CLEARLY DISTINCT?

Techniques for *keeping your head together* about which hat you are wearing—and when—range widely. At one extreme, there are those who are absolutely unyielding in their refusal to discuss their job with AA members or at an AA meeting (and vice versa). At the other extreme, there are those who talk easily about both in all settings, but always use some simple qualification. For example: "As an AA member, I feel so-and-so, but as a professional person, I would recommend such and such . . ."

Several AAs wrote, "From 9 to 5 on my job, I am a paid professional. But after hours, I turn into just another drunk trying to stay sober in AA."

A majority of our respondents seemed to feel that what is needed most is quiet common sense—*provided* you approach each situation on its own merits, *provided* you are deeply acquainted with AA Traditions and their application, and *provided* you watch your language very carefully.

"I never *sponsor* or *12th step* the *clients* I meet on my job," one counselor wrote. "I *counsel* them and arrange for other AAs to do the 12th stepping.

"But at my AA meetings, I 12th step pigeons like everyone else—being careful, of course, not to confuse my pigeons and my clients."

"And in AA, I am careful to avoid all professional-sounding jargon."

One popular AA speaker said, "In AA, I prefer to speak only as an AA member about my own subjective experience with alcoholism and recovery. If specifically asked to do so, however, I will talk to AA groups about my work; but I insist that it be announced *in advance* that I am *not* there as an AA speaker, but in my non-AA job role. This helps eliminate disappointment or misunderstandings."

Another declines to speak in her *professional* capacity at any AA meeting in her home community. "Here," she wrote, "I just use my name with no job title, and tell my AA story at AA meetings. I prefer to reserve my professional hat for professional occasions, mostly in other parts of the country."

Another member, a doctor, does just the opposite. He speaks in hometown meetings strictly as a guest professional, never mentioning his own AA membership except when far from home.

Nearly all the two-hatters emphasized that the biggest reason for keeping the two identities distinct is protection of your *own* recovery. "I cannot afford to start mistaking my professional work with alcoholics for the healing process provided me by the AA Steps and meetings," as one explained.

WHAT OTHER TRAPS CAN ALCOHOLISM JOBS SOMETIMES SET FOR AA'S?

1. *Recurring ego inflation—especially if you begin to see good results on your job*—was warned about. "Humility and gratitude are not only more becoming; they are also much safer, more in line with AA teachings, and far more helpful in my own growth," one member summarized.

Another wrote, "Try never to feel or sound like an expert on AA at either your home AA group or on your job. And try to avoid thinking or acting like an expert on alcoholism both at AA meetings and in professional non-AA circles.

"If you come on like an expert on either," he said, "you antagonize both your professional colleagues and your fellow AAs. Anyhow, aren't bar rooms already filled with enough experts on AA?"

2. *Failure to give credit and praise to non-AA pro's* who do perform services for alcoholics is also an easy mistake to lapse into. "Everyone deserves and needs sincere appreciation. I have

found that being liberal with praise—just a decent human courtesy—helps foster a climate of friendliness and cooperation."

3. *Getting impatient with and criticizing the ideas, practices, and attitudes of non-AAs* whose ideas are different from your own is a corollary danger respondents warned about.

"It does absolutely no good, makes your own job harder, and creates enemies for AA," the assistant director of a large institute wrote.

"By all means curb your eager-beaver impulses to keep ramming AA down everybody's throat. Never get trapped into arguments about AA and avoid the inclination to try to defend, explain, or interpret AA. The Fellowship's results speak eloquently for themselves. Clam up and let them," he said. "Don't brag about AA or make big claims about its success or its being the only or whole answer.

"If and when your non-AA colleagues do express any interest, take them or encourage them to go to AA meetings, or offer them one simple pamphlet such as "AA In Your Community" or "AA Wants to Work With You," or that famous all-medical issue of the Grapevine (October, 1968).

"And never say, *I told you so*. Do your own job well and let AA justify itself. It is not your job to turn the whole alcoholism world into AA fans; nor, is it your responsibility to make all AAs love the health professionals!" he warned.

WHAT ABOUT FUND RAISING, RESEARCH, AND THE WORLD DIRECTORY?

Experience has shown that these three subjects can cause misunderstandings between AA and the professional world. However, as many long-time two-hatters have shown, such problems can easily be solved, if not avoided.

1. *Fund Raising.* If the names of widely known AAs appear in connection with fund appeals, this is sometimes misinterpreted to mean that AA itself is seeking donations, or that AA *endorses* the organization asking for money.

According to Tradition No. 7, no AA office or group ever accepts money or gifts from non-AA sources. In accord with

Traditions No. 6 and No. 10, AA is not allied with and does not endorse or oppose any other organization or program.

AAs who understand the reasons for and principles behind these Traditions can prevent many troubles. See pages 159-169 and 180-183 in TWELVE STEPS AND TWELVE TRADITIONS and pages 30-208 in AA COMES OF AGE.

2. *Research.* When a professional agency wants to use AA members in research projects, it can be ticklish. Some AA members are disinterested in alcoholism research, and some even fear that such research could publicize their AA membership. Some professional agencies do not yet understand AAs primary purpose, or that no AA office, group, or any other unit can require AA members to do anything!

However, a number of worthwhile research projects involving AA members as *private citizens* have been accomplished when properly prepared for. Here at G.S.O. we can put you in touch with professional researchers who have successfully completed such projects without violations of AA Tradition and without offense.

3. *World Directory.* Because this annual booklet contains full names, addresses, and telephone numbers of AA members, it is for the eyes of AA members only and is not supposed to be shown or given to *any* non-AA.

It is labeled *CONFIDENTIAL* as a promise of privacy to those who permit their names to appear in it. Here at G.S.O. we are pledged to live up to that trust.

Of course, any AA member can have a Directory by ordering it through his own AA group, or by ordering it directly from P.O. Box 459, Grand Central Station, New York, New York, 10017. You must write on non-agency stationery, and give the name of your AA group.

At the direction and discretion of delegates to the General Service Conference, the Directory can also be made available to a few agencies that use it strictly to make referrals to AA, such as rehabilitation centers and rest homes.

Procedure prescribed by the Conference is this: the official agency request (which must be repeated every year) is referred to the delegate of the state where the agency is located. The delegate then decides whether or not the agency will make proper use of the Directory.

As you can see, these precautions are necessary to prevent improper use of the Directory and to prevent its falling into unauthorized hands. If we here at G.S.O. simply supplied the Directory willy-nilly to anyone who offered to buy it, we would betray the confidence of many members who trust us not to reveal their names and membership.

The purpose of the Directory is to enable AA members to get in touch with each other in regard to AA matters only, and to facilitate referrals of alcoholics to AA, especially in distant areas.

WHAT ABOUT ANONYMITY?

Saying, "*I am in AA*" or otherwise revealing your own AA membership, using full name and/or identifiable photo, is a violation of our Tradition No. 11 *only when it is done at the level of print, TV, radio, films or other public media.* None of our respondents even remotely favored changing or altering this Tradition in any way. No one even hinted that it is ever all right to violate it under any circumstances.

(The values of this Tradition for individual recovery, as well as protection of our Fellowship, are clearly spelled out in AA COMES OF AGE, TWELVE STEPS AND TWELVE TRADITIONS, and the leaflet, *Why Alcoholics Anonymous is Anonymous.*)

No respondent questioned our ethical responsibility *never* to reveal the AA membership, or alcoholism, of any *other* AA. (Just as no one questions the privileged, confidential nature of the doctor-patient, lawyer-client, priest-parishioner relationships.) As you know, AA publications, offices, groups, and committees make every effort NEVER to reveal in any way the identity of another AA member.

However, whether or not you disclose your *own* AA membership is your own affair; and if you do, it does not violate the Eleventh Tradition *as long as you do not do it in the public media.*

It has always been left strictly up to your own desires and judgment to decide about telling family, friends, employer, or colleagues . . . in   private conversations, in speaking engagements, or when trying to help an alcoholic into AA. It still is.

No Tradition explicitly covers this kind of *personal* communication. In fact, the fifth, ninth, and twelfth steps specifically suggest that we *do* tell people how we are trying to help ourselves recover. Such private revelations are built into our recovery program. Everyone of us when we first approach AA is 12th stepped by someone who tells honestly and openly of his or her own alcoholism, and recovery in AA. No AA Tradition or custom has ever suggested that it is good for an AA to *hide* his illness or *keep secret* his recovery from it. We are not ashamed of being recovered alcoholics.

AN ENTIRELY DIFFERENT MATTER, of course, is *saying publicly in print, on TV or anywhere else, simply, "I am a recovered alcoholic."* This statement alone is never a break of any AA Tradition—as long as *AA membership* is not *broadcast* or *published.*

Most respondents understand the difference, and scrupulously respect the 11th Tradition.

So, even though it is perfectly okay (a) to say *anywhere,* "I am a recovered alcoholic," and (b) even to reveal AA membership *on a personal basis,* we found a wide range of thoughtful opinion on when and where it is a good idea to do either of these.

Some respondents said they often identify themselves simply as *recovered alcoholics* because this may help chip away at the stigma surrounding alcoholism, and in the long-run may contribute to changing the stereotype of the alcoholic and attitudes toward alcoholics.

On the other hand, other respondents pointed out a disadvantage. They said if it is known you are a former victim of active alcoholism you are immediately viewed in some circles as a *special pleader with a vested interest,* and this may lessen your influence as a supposedly objective, professional person. In some cases, it was pointed out, when your alcoholism history becomes known you are, alas, still a subject of distrust and suspicion from some people.

Aside from strict adherence to Tradition No. 11, and to a policy of *never* revealing either alcoholism or AA membership of anyone *else*, practically no one recommended setting up a rigid policy for yourself and never deviating from it no matter what the circumstances.

"Consider in each instance to whom you are talking, under what circumstances, for what purpose, and in which role," one man wrote. "Consider the possible benefits or harm that can be done over the long haul. Talking at a professional gathering, or on a radio show or newspaper interview, it may, or may not, be a good idea to say that you are a recovered alcoholic.

"Speaking to a troubled alcoholic client, maybe you could help him with your own story—but it is also possible this might hinder his own affiliation with AA. He may not understand your motive.

"Remember that what you do can affect yourself, your listener, and AA as a whole for years to come," he advised. "To sum up, I'd say examine your conscience fearlessly, then pray for guidance in each case."

Maybe you would also profit by discussing specific instances with other AAs who have faced such questions. And you are certainly urged to write or telephone the Professional Relations Secretary at G.S.O. if you think we can be of any assistance.

MISCELLANEOUS SUGGESTIONS

From the wealth of good experience shared with us, we've also culled a few miscellaneous tips you might find helpful:

1. Remember that *your* basic training in alcoholism is subjective, personal experience. Non-AAs naturally have to see the illness objectively, from other, outer directions, not from the inside. "This does not necessarily mean one view is better than the other," one man wrote. "They are *different,* but both can be true, good and helpful to the sick alcoholic."

2. Be sure to maintain, outside, or in addition to your job, a personal AA life of your own.

3. Go regularly to AA meetings not as a guest expert or big shot, but as a *listening newcomer* trying to stay sober. It's fun!

4. Never be afraid to say you are wrong, you're sorry, you don't know, you goofed, or you need help.

5. If your job threatens your sobriety, by all means get out of it. The alcoholism business is not the right vocation for everybody, in AA or out of it. And *no* job is as important as your sobriety.

6. If you speak as an AA member, be sure to emphasize that you speak only for yourself, since *no* AA member can speak for or represent AA as a whole.

WHAT HAS AA HISTORY SHOWN ABOUT AA'S IN ALCOHOLISM JOBS?

For more than twenty-five years AA members have been working professionally in the field of alcoholism. Our co-founder, Dr. Bob S., in addition to his personal AA 12th stepping, also treated alcoholics in his professional capacity as a physician. Marty M. pioneered in 1944 in starting to educate the public about alcoholism. She had the full support of Dr. Bob, Bill W., and other early AAs. They say then that the organizing and fund-raising necessary for public education on alcoholism were outside AAs ability and primary purpose.

By 1957, as Bill W. pointed out in AA COMES OF AGE, many AAs were already successfully employed to work on alcoholism problems by non-AA organizations in such capacities as social workers, researchers, educators, nurses, personnel advisors, rehabilitation farm managers and many others.

Looking back, we can clearly see now that it would be unreasonable and futile to try to prevent AA members from using any professional skills they have in institutions and programs concerned with alcoholism. Many AAs have now made remarkable professional contributions to the world's knowledge and understanding of alcoholism, while acting fully within both the letter and spirit of the AA Traditions. It *can* be done; it *has* been done.

In addition to being good AA members, carrying the AA message of recovery freely to other alcoholics—many professional men and women who are members of AA have also, as individuals, used their non-AA expertise as psychiatrists, fund raisers, psychologists, corrections officers, jurists, and counselors to help alcoholism agencies and facilities perform for alcoholics many of the vital services which AA cannot and does not offer victims of alcoholism. They give medical and legal aid, feed, clothe, shelter, perform research, provide vocational aid, public education, community organization, etc.

"We see that we have no right or need to discourage AAs who wish to work as individuals in these wider fields," according to Bill W. (AA COMES OF AGE—page 117). "It would be actually anti-social were we to discourage them."

Chapter XII

ALCOHOLICS ANONYMOUS TRAINING GROUPS

A Suggested Group Format To Be Used By The Para-professional

Leona M. Kent

Several years ago, while I was working as a para-professional in an outpatient clinic, I wrote a paper titled THE UTILIZATION OF ALCOHOLICS ANONYMOUS TRAINING GROUPS IN A CLINIC SETTING.

Much to my surprise the paper was so well received that requests for copies started coming in from all over the country. Later, largely through the efforts of John L. Norris, M.D., nonalcoholic chairman of the AA General Service Board, a shortened version of the paper was published in the March, 1969 issue of the *Grapevine*, the International Monthly Journal of Alcoholics Anonymous. Later in that same year, I presented the paper to the clinical symposium at the North American Association of Alcoholism Programs' annual meeting.*

As a result of this exposure, more and more requests began pouring in from as far away as Australia and New Zealand and as close to home as my community itself. To this date there is rarely a week goes by that one or two requests are not received.

Many people wrote asking how they could go about setting up an AA Training Group. It became apparent that there was a

---

* 20th Annual Meeting, Vancouver, British Columbia, September, 1969.

need to develop a model which would provide guidelines for those who wanted to implement a similar program.

Today, the *Model for Alcoholics Anonymous Training Groups* is being widely used, not only in outpatient clinics but also in institutions, inpatient facilities and halfway houses.

The remainder of this chapter will consist of the greater part of both of these papers. It is being reproduced in the hope that it will be helpful and informative to those who seek a way to implement in their own programs a method of bridging the gap which exists between the professional and para-professional, while leading to a fuller understanding of the philosophy of Alcoholics Anonymous.

AA TRAINING GROUPS IN A CLINIC SETTING

To provide the most effective means of recovery to the alcoholic, regardless of approach, would seem to be the most logical goal of all those who are working in a professional capacity in the field of alcoholism.

Too much valuable time is being wasted in useless criticisms of and jealousy between professionals and individual members of Alcoholics Anonymous. Why does this mistrust and lack of understanding continue to exist? There are a number of reasons.

Although Alcoholics Anonymous is often used as a dumping ground for the client who does not fit the agency model, it is seldom used initially or integrated into a plan for rehabilitation. Similarly, clinics are often used by the members of AA as a dropping off place for those who are without funds or for detoxification purposes only. This behavior in itself serves to broaden the gap which already exists between professionals and AAs.

Too often the emphasis is placed on the differences between the two approaches with almost complete disregard for their similarities.

Too often the professional believes the attitude of an individual AA member to be representative of the average member. It may, in fact, be representative only of the uninformed professional, whose knowledge of the Alcoholics Anonymous program is meager, or frequently nonexistent.

One might ask, are these individuals in the minority? I believe they are. On the inside cover of an official Alcoholics Anonymous pamphlet, entitled *Cooperation not Affiliation* which is distributed by the General Service Office of Alcoholics Anonymous, there is a statement which reads as follows: "Alcoholics Anonymous acknowledges its debt to all the men and women who are engaged in studying and treating the victims of alcoholism. Without this help many of us would not be alive today." There are large numbers of AA members who are working in a professional capacity within industry, state and local agencies and in the field of education and there are hundreds of professionally trained people who are devoting full time to using their own particular skills to help the alcoholic, not only in treatment but in research and education and in establishing alcoholism programs.

Numerous articles have been written about the advantages which would be realized if AA-professional relationships were improved. Dr. Milton Maxwell, Executive Director of the Rutgers Summer School of Alcohol Studies, in his paper PROFESSIONAL AND ALCOHOLICS ANONYMOUS RELATIONS IN OREGON: An Exploratory Study Report, emphasizes the need for mutual understanding. He states:

> Not many AA's nor many professionals really know very much about each other. Not many AA's have any idea of what goes on in a professional clinic, and as the one AA who did know, said, "You can't tell them about it either; they have to participate to understand." Most professionals, similarly, know very little about AA, and as one professional said: "You can't tell another professional about AA; they've got to get acquainted and see for themselves."[1]

How can we begin to stimulate enough interest so that professionals and AAs will consciously strive for a better understanding of each other? I propose that one way to accomplish this is by

---

[1] Milton A. Maxwell: *Professional and Alcoholic Anonymous Relations in Oregon: An Exploratory Study Report.* State of Oregon Mental Health Division, Alcohol Studies and Rehabilitation Section, p. 8.

effectively coordinating the two approaches into a rehabilitation plan.

It is important to emphasize that coordinating the two approaches in no way implies a combination of approaches nor does it suggest a desertion of either. Each stands on its own merit, but with coordination there is an implicit understanding that each approach is aware of its own limitations, thereby allowing everyone involved in treatment to provide those services which he is best qualified to provide. Marty Mann in her *New Primer on Alcoholism* points out:

> In alcoholic clinics already functioning or being planned, psychiatric diagnosis and treatment are an important part of their services; of equal importance is the active cooperation of successful members of Alcoholics Anonymous. Each has something to contribute which the other needs, if they are able to help more alcoholics more successfully. Working together, they can be expected to return more alcoholics to sober, happy lives, *and to keep them there*, than either could do alone. The problem of alcoholism is serious and difficult enough to insist upon the fullest and widest use of everything that has ever proved helpful.[2]

Before describing an AA training group let us first look at how this plan was conceived and developed.

Clinics rarely see successful members of Alcoholics Anonymous. Rather, their exposure is to those individuals who have been unable to accept the philosophy of AA or apply it to their own lives. It is not at all unusual during the intake process to have a client make derogatory statements in reference to AA. Remarks such as *that bunch of phonies!, who wants to sit around and listen to people talk about their drinking?, all AA ever did for me was make me thirsty* are frequent. It becomes apparent to one who is familiar with the philosophy of the AA program that these individuals are reacting personally to individual AA members. They have a personalized view of AA but have little or no knowledge of the philosophy which is contained in the twelve steps of the AA program.

---

[2] Marty Mann: *New Primer on Alcoholism*. New York: Holt, Rinehart and Winston, p. 154, 1966.

On the basis of psychological testing and counselor evaluation, we frequently find individuals who show limited insight and little or no sophistication for whom AA would be the preferred treatment recommendation. Often, these are the very individuals who have rejected AA, or have been dismissed by individual members of AA as *not being ready*. In an effort to overcome the obstacles which presented themselves to these clients the idea of an AA training group was born. Why not form a group in the clinic which would stress the philosophy of AA? It seemed reasonable to assume that a group such as this could effectively coordinate the methods of Alcoholics Anonymous and group counseling. Preparations for the forming of an AA training group to be conducted by a staff member who was also a member of Alcoholics Anonymous were begun. As a precaution against alienating AA in the community, the idea was presented to the AA General Service Headquarters in New York, and it was ascertained that the forming of this group would in no way violate AA tradition. While the plans were being developed, more ways in which the group could be utilized presented themselves.

The training group could provide not only the opportunity to coordinate the use of AA into a rehabilitation plan, thereby improving AA professional relationships, but could also enable a staff member to evaluate an individual for possible movement into a psychotherapeutically oriented group within the clinic.

By placing three categories of individuals in AA training groups, the following hypothetical assumptions were made:

1. If the AA drop-out is placed in a training group for a specified number of weeks it may be possible to re-educate him in the use of the AA philosophy.
2. If the individual with little or no knowledge of AA is placed in a training group and provided with a basic knowledge of the philosophy of the AA program, the possibility of his becoming an AA drop-out will be considerably lessened.
3. If the nonverbal, confused alcoholic is placed in a training group, it is possible he will develop the insight necessary to be moved into a psychotherapeutically oriented group, while at the same time continuing to use the AA program as an integral part of his treatment.

After the client completed a diagnostic and evaluation period the clinic staff met for case conference to determine which method of treatment was indicated for the individual. Primarily, decisions were made on the basis of counselor evaluation, results of psychological testing, contributions of other members of the staff who came in contact with the client, psychiatric evaluation and medical information. If it was then decided that the treatment of choice was Alcoholics Anonymous, the client was assigned to twelve weeks in an AA training group.

The training group met in the conference room of the clinic. Here the setting can best be described as attractive and relaxed, the seating was comfortable and coffee available. Comments made by clients suggested that the alcoholic felt this was a special place which had been created with him in mind, a feeling of *this is my clinic.*

Group sessions were structured around a pamphlet entitled *An Interpretation of the Twelve Steps,* which divides the AA program into four phases: admission, spiritual, inventory, and restitution and action. In twelve weeks the four phases were repeated three times. This was done so all of the essentials of the twelve steps were covered and the alcoholic became familiar with them.

The twelve steps of the AA program are as follows:

1. We admitted we were powerless over alcohol; that our lives had become unmanageable.
2. Came to believe that a power greater than ourselves could restore us to sanity.
3. Made a decision to turn our will and our lives over to the care of God *as we understood Him.*
4. Made a searching and fearless moral inventory of ourselves.
5. Admitted to God, to ourselves and to another human being the exact nature of our wrongs.
6. Were entirely ready to have God remove all these defects of character.
7. Humbly asked Him to remove our shortcomings.
8. Made a list of all persons we had harmed, and became willing to make amends to them all.
9. Made direct amends to such people wherever possible, except when to do so would injure them or others.

10. Continue to take personal inventory and when we were wrong, promptly admitted it.
11. Sought through prayer and meditation to improve our conscious contact with God *as we understood Him,* praying only for knowledge of His will for us and the power to carry that out.
12. Having had a spiritual experience as the result of these steps, we tried to carry this message to alcoholics and practice these principles in all our affairs.

The group discussion on *admission* covered the first step of the AA program. During this session questions such as *What is an alcoholic, who is an alcoholic, am I an alcoholic, and why does an alcoholic drink?"* were discussed. Test questions which have been used as a guide by Johns Hopkins University Hospital in deciding whether a patient is alcoholic or not, were reviewed and each member was helped to determine for himself whether he is an alcoholic.

Discussion number two, *the spiritual phase,* covered steps 2, 3, 5, 6, 7, and 11. Any discussion of the spiritual phase of the AA program is meaningless until each group member can determine in his own mind his definition of *spiritual.* The obstacles which present themselves to the agnostic, athiest, or the individual who has had continuing but unsatisfying church affiliations, since he has been unable to implement the philosophy of his religion in his personal life, were brought into the open and freely discussed.

Discussion number three, *inventory and restitution,* covered steps 4, 8, 9, and 10. Here the alcoholic was encouraged to evaluate himself honestly, not using professional terminology but as a person who needs a basic understanding of the nature of his illness. He begins to realize that full rehabilitation is the objective, that sobriety for sobriety's sake is not enough, and that reservations defeat this purpose.

Discussion number four, *action,* covers the twelfth step. This step logically separates into three parts, spiritual experience, carry the message, and practice the principles. For the purposes of the session, they were covered as such. The major emphasis of the session is usually, but need not be, spiritual experience, *what is it?*

At the first meeting of the AA training group a contract is made between the members of the group and the leader. It is established that each person understands that he has been assigned to the group for a specified period of twelve weeks and will then be referred to AA in the community. Rules of the group are clearly stated. *Drunkalogues* are not allowed and an explanation of the term is given. A *drunkalogue* is a description of a drinking experience detailed to the extent of including the kind and quantity of alcoholic beverage consumed. In line with the AA concept that it may be therapeutic, however, a drinking experience which is significant to the individual may be related. Assurance is given that no one is required to state he is an alcoholic, although he may do so if he chooses. This is one of the most frequent objections to community AA groups as expressed by the AA drop-out. The fact that the vast majority of AAs preface their remarks by stating their name, followed by the phrase *I am an alcoholic,* implies to these individuals that it is a requirement of AA membership. Permission is given to those who have negative feelings about AA to talk about them. One might easily describe this first session as a *gripe* session and it is perhaps one of the most beneficial for the leader as it reveals to him each individual's objection to the AA program.

Every group session is started with the leader reading the format for a specific discussion as contained in the pamphlet AN INTERPRETATION OF THE TWELVE STEPS. At the conclusion of the reading the group then discusses the material which has been presented. They are encouraged to interact and they soon realize that they may openly disagree with an individual without evoking the disapproval of the leader or the other group members.

It would be well at this point to examine the differences between AA in the community and the training group. Although there is a variation from one group to another, typically, community AA stresses the fellowship of AA and minimizes its philosophy thereby creating fertile ground for personal issues to emerge. By shifting the emphasis from the fellowship to the philosophy, personality conflicts are not likely to present themselves. Implicit rules in many community AA groups have a limiting effect on the individual's freedom to interpret AA philosophy as he chooses, without provoking the group's disapproval, resulting in their strong pressure for him to conform or be rejected. Rules in the training group are explicit. Large numbers tend to restrict interaction and with this in mind the number in the training group is controlled, with a minimum of four and a maximum of ten. Outside of an occasional closed group in the community where interaction does take place, the typical AA group is composed of a chairman who leads the meeting and calls on each individual to speak. Traditionally, each member speaks as suggested in the fifth chapter of the book *Alcoholics Anonymous*: "our stories disclose in a general way, what we used to be like, what happened, and what we are like now."[3]

In an official AA pamphlet entitled "Is AA for You?" it is stated, "Our primary purpose is to stay sober and help other alcoholics achieve sobriety." This is perhaps the most significant difference between the training groups and Alcoholics Anonymous as a whole. The training group has a number of goals. The immediate one is, of course, sobriety but there are other goals of a broader scope. They may be outlined as follows:

1. To lessen the number of AA drop-outs.
2. To coordinate the methods of AA and the professional.
3. To provide a basic knowledge of AA philosophy and encourage each individual to become affiliated with AA so they may have a lifetime program.
4. To improve AA-professional relationships through mutual understanding.
5. To evaluate the individual so those who need professional help might be placed in a counseling group.

Results of the training group were very positive. Many AA drop-outs returned to AA. Professionals furthered their understanding of AA and were more willing to refer and refer more appropriately. Clients who were initially evaluated as not being reachable through the traditional clinical methods were found

---

[3] Anonymous: *Alcoholics Anonymous*, New York, Alcoholics Anonymous World Services, Inc., p. 58, 1955.

to be good candidates for group counseling. So much enthusiasm was generated by the first clients who completed twelve weeks of AA training that they started their own closed interaction AA group in the community. They continued to accept referrals from the training group.

The AA training group is a simple program designed to meet the needs of those alcoholics who for a variety of reasons have been unable to accept the AA program. The format is such that any AA member can present it, provided he does not hold the idea that only an alcoholic can help an alcoholic or that the AA program is the only answer for all alcoholics.

What is the feasibility of having training groups in other places and in other settings? No difficulties presented themselves which would by any means discourage others from repeating this elsewhere. If this is done, an alliance can be established between professionals and AA members so they can work together, each with his own methods and in his own area.

No one has all the answers. Each approach has its successes and its failures but sharing the responsibilities for the treatment of the alcoholic is one sure way of accomplishing the common goal of helping more alcoholics return to normal, useful lives.

THE MODEL

The following pages contain some guide lines to those who are interested in starting an AA training group. The emphasis is being placed on the utilization of these groups in a professional setting, but may well be adapted for use in a closed AA group.

The basic material which was used in the first training group can be found in the appendix. The majority of the material was from the pamphlet *An Interpretation of the Twelve Steps,* author unknown, publisher unknown.

A pamphlet entitled *The Tablemate,* A guide to the Study of the Twelve Steps, Amity Press, Tacoma, Washington (no longer in existence), contains similar material. In this pamphlet, however, much of the ritual to which the AA drop-out objects is included and could be a deterrent to the effectiveness of the training group.

THE GROUP LEADER

The group leader should be a member of Alcoholics Anonymous who has been able to internalize the philosophy of the twelve steps of the AA program and is able to set a good example of complete sobriety. He must be knowledgeable, not only about AA, but also about alcoholism as a whole, as he may find himself in a position where he will be required to provide answers to pertinent questions. We are all aware that no one speaks for AA, but in this particular setting, we must face the fact that the group leader is representative of AA.

Since the AA training group is designed to meet the needs of those individuals who have been unable to use the AA program as a means of recovery, it is essential that the group leader be open-minded. Any indication that he is of the opinion that AA is the *only* answer for *all* alcoholics will only alienate the professional staff of the clinic.

The first step is to allow each individual the freedom to speak openly and honestly about his feelings in reference to AA. Whether these feelings are positive or negative is irrelevant. For the most part, in a clinic setting they are negative.

To provide an environment where problems can be brought into the open and freely discussed is a function of the group. Only by allowing this, can the newcomer be encouraged to remove some of the stumbling blocks which have prevented him from using the twelve steps as a program of recovery.

Many times observations made by the newcomer are in direct conflict with the leader's personal experience and one needs to know that to advise or show disapproval at this point can only serve to reinforce the feelings of *conform or be rejected* which are already a part of the drop-out's experience. Either by inference or in actuality, the temptation is to convey the message *do as I do.* This must be avoided.

The leader must give some consideration to his own role in the group. He must recognize that he is not a teacher nor an advisor, although he does direct and challenge. Most important of all, he is the symbol of a sober, healthy individual who lets the group know he does care about them and what happens to them. This demonstration of warmth and understanding permits each group member to find his own way and gives him permission to apply the principles of the twelve steps to his own life as he chooses.

INTRODUCTION TO THE GROUP

When a group meets for the first time, the leader describes the function of the group and the outline of the program as it is presented. A contract between the group members and the leader is established so that each person understands he will be expected to attend the group for twelve weeks. The leader may wish to elaborate on the importance of consistent attendance, but must be cautious so that he does not infer attendance is mandatory.

It is the responsibility of the leader to point out the differences between the training group and groups in the community. If this is not done, the group assumes that the leader will call on each person to speak, thereby defeating one of the purposes of the training group by discouraging interaction.

Rules of the group are outlined. Since one of the reasons most often given for not attending AA meetings seems to be an objection to hearing about drinking, the group is given the responsibility to confront any member who goes into detail about his drinking. The leader assumes the right to determine when the relating of a drinking experience may be therapeutic for the individual concerned.

Shifting the emphasis from the fellowship to the philosophy of AA could present problems if the leader does not exercise good judgment in presenting this idea. *We are not seeking to underestimate the value of the fellowship,* only attempting to break down the barrier which has been set up by so many who have allowed their reaction to individual AA members to interfere with their learning of AA principles. Many of these people, once they have acquired an understanding of the basic principles of the AA program, are able to differentiate between the two.

Many AA members who have returned to drinking have been dismissed by their group as not ready. In the training group, we consider the possibility that some individuals need to be prepared before they are able to accept the program. Hopefully, after twelve weeks of preparation, some of these people will be able to attend AA meetings in the community with a more favorable attitude.

CONCLUSION

The great need of our time is the willingness of all who are involved in the treatment of the alcoholic to pool their resources and abilities by working together on a cooperative basis.

All professional and para-professional disciplines have much to offer and are doing so in treatment centers all over the world and Alcoholics Anonymous continues to grow and gain stature over the years. Surely mutual respect and understanding can only lead to more and better services for the alcoholic.

When invited to read a paper on the Fellowship of Alcoholics Anonymous to the American Psychiatric Association, Bill W. AA's co-founder, concluded his talk with an appeal: "We of AA try to be aware that we may never touch but a segment of the total alcoholic problem. We try to remember that our growing success may prove a heady wine; that our own resources will always be limited. So, then, will you men and women of medicine be our partners, physicians wielding well your invisible scalpels, workers all in our common cause?"

FORMAT
FOR USE IN ALCOHOLICS ANONYMOUS
TRAINING GROUPS

Meetings Number 1, 5, 9

ADMISSION

This meeting covers Step No. 1. *We admitted we were powerless over alcohol, that our lives had become unmanageable.*

In order to determine whether or not a person has drifted from *social drinking* into pathological drinking, it is well to check over a list of test questions which each member may ask himself and answer for himself.

We must answer once and for all these three puzzling questions:

What is an alcoholic?
Who is an alcoholic?
Am I an alcoholic?

To get the right answer, the prospective member must start this course of instruction with:

1. A willingness to learn. We must not have the attitude of *you've got to show me.*
2. An open mind. Forget any and all ideas or notions we already have. Set our opinions aside.
3. Complete honesty. It is possible, not at all probable, that we may fool somebody else. But we MUST be honest with ourselves, and it is a good time to start being honest with others.

SUGGESTED TEST QUESTIONS

NOTE: These questions are not AA questions. They are guides which have been used by John Hopkins University Hospital in deciding whether a patient is alcoholic or not.

1. Do you require a drink the next morning?
2. Do you prefer to drink alone?
3. Do you lose time from work due to drinking?
4. Is your drinking harming your family in any way?
5. Do you crave a drink at a definite time daily?
6. Do you get the inner shakes unless you continue drinking?
7. Has drinking made you irritable?
8. Does drinking make you careless of your family's welfare?
9. Have you harmed your husband or wife since drinking?
10. Has drinking changed your personality?
11. Does drinking cause you bodily complaints?
12. Does drinking make you restless?
13. Does drinking cause you to have difficulty in sleeping?
14. Has drinking made you more impulsive?
15. Have you less self-control since drinking?

16. Has your initiative decreased since drinking?
17. Has your ambition decreased since drinking?
18. Do you lack perserverance in pursuing a goal since drinking?
19. Do you drink to obtain social ease? (In shy, timid, self-counscious individuals.)
20. Do you drink for self-encouragement? (In persons with feelings of inferiority.)
21. Do you drink to relieve marked feelings of inadequacy?
22. Has your sexual potency suffered since drinking?
23. Do you show marked dislikes and hatreds since drinking?
24. Has your jealousy, in general, increased since drinking?
25. Do you show marked moodiness as a result of drinking?
26. Has your efficiency decreased since drinking?
27. Has your drinking made you more sensitive?
28. Are you harder to get along with since drinking?
29. Do you turn to an inferior environment since drinking?
30. Is drinking endangering your health?
31. Is drinking affecting your peace of mind?
32. Is drinking making your home life unhappy?
33. Is drinking jeopardizing your business?
34. Is drinking clouding your reputation?
35. Is drinking disturbing the harmony of your life?

In addition to the test questions, we in AA would ask even more questions. Here are a few:

36. Have you ever had a complete loss of memory while, or after drinking?
37. Have you ever felt, when or after drinking, an inability to concentrate?
38. Have you ever felt remorse after drinking?
39. Has a physician ever treated you for drinking?
40. Have you ever been hospitalized for drinking?

If you have answered YES to any *one* of the Test Questions, there is a definite warning that you *may* be alcoholic. If you answered YES to any *two* of the Test Questions, the chances are that you *are* an alcoholic.

If you answer YES to *three* or more of the Test Questions, you are *definitely* AN ALCOHOLIC.

WHY DOES AN ALCOHOLIC DRINK?

Having decided that we are alcoholics, it is well to consider what competent mental doctors consider as the REASONS why an Alcoholic drinks.

1. As an escape from situations of life which he cannot face.
2. As evidence of a maladjusted personality (including sexual maladjustments).
3. As a development from social drinking to pathological drinking.
4. As a symptom of a major abnormal mental state.
5. As an escape from incurable physical pain.
6. Because of basic feelings of inferiority—emotional instability—a sick personality. A person who drinks because he likes alcohol, knows he cannot handle it (but does not care), is considered emotionally unstable.
7. Usually one cannot pinpoint any glaring reason why the alcoholic drinks. In most cases it is more than a suspicion that the alcohol is consumed to relieve a vague restlessness or boredom. The liquid escape temporarily lessens the conflict between physical and emotional networks and the ordinary strains of life.

The above are general reasons. Where the individuality or personality of the alcoholic is concerned, these reasons may be divided as follows:

1. A self-pampering tendency which manifests itself in refusal to tolerate, even temporarily, unpleasant states of mind such as boredom, sorrow, anger, disappointment, worry, depression, dissatisfaction and feelings of inferiority and inadequacy. *I want what I want when I want it* seems to express the attitude of many alcoholics toward life.
2. An instinctive urge for self-expression, unaccompanied by determination to translate the urge into creative action.
3. An abnormal craving for emotional experiences which calls for removal of intellectual restraint.
4. Powerful hidden ambitions without the necessary resolve

to attain them, coupled with discontent, irritability, depression, disgruntlesness and general restlessness.

5. A tendency to flinch from the worries of life and to seek escape from reality by the easiest means available.
6. An unreasonable demand for continuous happiness or excitement.
7. An insistent craving for the feeling of self-confidence, calm and poise that some obtain temporarily from alcohol.

WE ADMIT

If after carefully considering the foregoing, we ADMIT we are alcoholic, we must realize that—

Once a person becomes a pathological drinker, he can never again become a controlled drinker; and from that point on, is limited to just two alternatives:

1. Total permanent abstinence.
2. Chronic alcoholism with all of the handicaps and penalties it implies. In other words, we have gone past the point where we HAD A CHOICE.

All we have left is a DECISION to make.

WE RESOLVE TO DO SOMETHING ABOUT IT

1. WE MUST CHANGE OUR WAY OF THINKING. (This is such an important matter that it will have to be more fully discussed later.)
2. We resolve that we will practice AA for the twenty-four hours of that day.
3. We must study the other eleven Steps of the Program, and practice each and every one.
4. Attend the regular Group Meeting each week without fail.
5. Firmly believe that by practicing AA faithfully each day, we will achieve sobriety.
6. Believe that we can be free from alcohol as a problem.
7. Contact another member BEFORE taking a drink, tell him what bothers you, talk it over with him freely. In most cases you will be spared the misery of a slip.

8. Work the Program for ourselves alone, not for our wife, children, friends or for our job.
9. Be absolutely honest and sincere.
10. Be fully open minded, no mental reservations.
11. Be fully willing to work the Program. Nothing good in life comes without work.

CONCLUSION

1. Alcoholics are suffering from a three fold illness: mental, physical and spiritual. Fortunately, we in AA have learned how it may be controlled (this will be shown in the next eleven Steps of the Program).
2. We can also learn to be FREE from alcohol as a problem.
3. We can achieve a full and happy life without recourse to alcohol.

Meetings Number 2, 6, 10.

THE SPIRITUAL

This meeting covers steps 2, 3, 5, 6, 7, and 11. We will take them in order.

STEP No. 2—*Came to believe that a Power greater than ourselves could restore us to sanity.*

Our drinking experience has shown—

1. That as we strayed away from the normal SOCIAL side of life, our minds became confused and we strayed away from the normal MENTAL side of life.
2. An abnormal MENTAL condition is certainly not SANITY in the accepted sense of the word. We have acquired or developed a MENTAL ILLNESS. Our study of AA shows that—
   a. In the MENTAL or tangible side of life we have lost touch with, or ignored, or have forgotten the SPIRIT-UAL values that give us the dignity of MAN as differentiated from the ANIMAL. We have fallen back upon the MATERIAL things of life and these have failed us. We have been groping in the dark.

b. No HUMAN agency, no SCIENCE or ART has been able to solve the alcoholic problem, so we turn to the SPIRITUAL for guidance.

Therefore, we *Come to believe that a Power greater than ourselves could restore us to sanity.*

STEP No. 3—*Make a decision to turn our will and our lives over to the care of GOD as we understand Him.* In the first step we learned that we had lost power of CHOICE and had to make a DECISION.

1. What better DECISION could we make than to turn our very WILL over to GOD, realizing that our own use of our own will had resulted in trouble.
2. God as we understand him.
3. RELIGION is a word we do not use in AA. We refer to a member's relation to GOD as the SPIRITUAL. A religion is a FORM of worship, not the workship itself.
4. If a man cannot believe in GOD he can certainly believe in SOMETHING greater than himself. If he cannot believe in a Power greater than himself, he is a rather hopeless egotist.

STEP No. 5—*Admitted to GOD, to ourselves and to another human being the exact nature of our wrongs.*

1. There is nothing new in this step. There are many sound reasons for *talking over our troubles out loud with others.* It is a natural human act to unburden ourselves.
2. The Catholic already has this medium readily available to him in the Confessional. But, the Catholic is at a disadvantage if he thinks his familiarity with confession permits him to think his part of AA is thereby automatically taken care of. He must, in confession, seriously consider his problems in relation to his alcoholic thinking.
3. The non-Catholic has the way open to work this step by going to his minister, his doctor, or his friend.
4. Under this step it is not even necessary to go to a priest or minister. Any understanding human being, friend or stranger will serve the purpose.

5. The purpose and intent of this step is so plain and definite that it needs little explanation. The point is that we MUST do EXACTLY what the Fifth Step says, sooner or later. We must not be in a rush to get this step off our chest. Consider it carefully and calmly. Then get about it and do it.

6. *Wrongs* do not necessarily mean *crime*. It can well be wrong thinking, selfishness, false pride, egotism, or any one of a hundred such negative faults.

STEP No. 6—*We're entirely ready to have God remove all these defects of character.*

1. After *admitting* our wrong thinking and wrong actions in Step 5, we now do something more than *admit* or *confess*.

2. We now become READY and WILLING to have God remove the defects in our CHARACTER.

3. Remember it is OUR character we are working on. Not the other fellow's. Here is a good place to drop the CRITICAL attitude toward others—the SUPERIOR attitude toward others.

4. We must clean our mind of wrong thinking, petty jealousy, envy, self-pity, remorse, etc.

5. Here is the place to drop RESENTMENTS, one of the biggest hurdles the alcoholic has to get over.

6. What concerns us here is that we drop all thoughts of resentment, anger, hatred, and revenge.

7. We turn our WILL over to God and let HIS WILL direct us how to patiently remove, one by one, all defects in our character.

STEP No. 7—*Humbly asked Him to remove our shortcomings.* The meaning of this step is clear. Prayer-Humility.

1. *Prayer.* No man can tell another HOW to pray. Each one has, or works out for himself, his own method. If we cannot pray, we just talk to God and tell Him our troubles. Meditate—think clearly and cleanly—and ask God to direct

our thoughts. If you cannot pray, ask God to teach you to pray.

2. *Humility.* This, simply, is the virtue of being ourselves and realizing how small we are in a big world full of its own trouble. Drop all pretense. We must not be Mr. Big Shot, bragging, boasting. Shed false pride. Tell the simple, plain, unvarnished truth. Act, walk and talk simply. See the little bit of good that exists in an evil man. Forget the little bit of evil that exists in the good man. We must not look down on the lowest of GOD's creatures or man's mistakes. Think clearly, honestly, fairly, generously.

3. The shortcomings we ask GOD to remove are the very defects in our character that make us drink. We drink to hide or to get away from these same defects.

STEP No. 11—*Sought through prayer and meditation to improve our conscious contact with GOD as we understand Him, praying only for knowledge of His will for us and the power to carry that out.*

1. We pray each night, every night, a prayer of thanks.
2. We pray each morning, every morning, for help and guidance.
3. When we are lonely, confused, uncertain, we pray.

Most of us find it well to:

1. Choose for each day, a *quiet time* to meditate on the Program, considering your progress in it.
2. Keep conscious contact with GOD and pray to make that contact closer.
3. Pray that our will be laid aside and that God's will direct us.
4. Pray for calmness, quiet, relaxation, rest.
5. Pray for strength and courage to enable us to do today's work today.
6. Pray for forgiveness for yesterday's errors.
7. Ask for HOPE for better things tomorrow.
8. Pray for what we feel we need. We will not get what we *want*. We will get what we *need*, what is good for us.

CONCLUSION

We find that no one need have difficulty with the spiritual side of the program. WILLINGNESS, HONESTY AND OPEN MINDEDNESS are the ESSENTIALS OF RECOVERY. THESE ARE INDISPENSABLE.

Meetings Number 3, 7, 11.

This meeting covers steps 4, 8, 9, 10. We will take them in order.

INVENTORY AND RESTITUTION

STEP No. 4—"*Made a searching and fearless moral inventory of ourselves.*" The intent and purpose of this step is plain. All alcoholics have a definite need for a good self-analysis, a sort of self-appraisal. Other people have certainly analyzed us, appraised us, criticized us and even judged us. It might be a good idea to judge ourselves, calmly and honestly.

We need inventory because—

1. Either our faults, weaknesses, defects of character—are the cause of our drinking OR—
2. Our drinking has weakened our character and let us drift into all kinds of wrong action, wrong attitudes, wrong viewpoints. In either event we obviously need an inventory and the only kind of inventory to make is a GOOD one. Moreover, the job is up to US. We created or we let develop all the anti-social actions that got US in wrong. So we have to work it out. WE must make a list of our faults and then we must do something about it.

The inventory must be four things—

1. It must be HONEST. Why waste time fooling ourselves with a phony list. We have fooled ourselves for years. We tried to fool others and now is a good time to look ourselves squarely in the eye.
2. It must be SEARCHING. Why skip over a vital matter lightly and quickly? Our trouble is a grave mental illness, confused by screwy thinking. Therefore, we must

SEARCH diligently and fearlessly to get at the TRUTH of what is wrong with us, just dig in and SEARCH.

3. It must be FEARLESS. We must not be afraid we might find things in our heart, mind and soul that we will hate to discover. If we do find such things they may be the ROOT of our trouble.

4. It must be a MORAL inventory. Some, in error, think the inventory is a lot of unpaid debts, plus a list of unmade apologies. Our trouble goes much deeper. We will find the root of our trouble lies in—

Resentments, false pride, envy, jealousy, selfishness and many other things. Laziness is important. In other words we are making an inventory of our character, our attitude toward others, our very way of living. Engaging in malicious gossip is a weakness of grave concern and requires honest self-evaluation to recognize and overcome. We are not preparing a financial statement. We will pay our bills because we cannot begin to practice the precepts of AA without HONESTY.

STEP No. 8—*Made a list of all persons we had harmed, and became willing to make amends to them all.* Under this step we will make a list (mental or written) of those we have harmed.

We ask GOD to let His Will be done, not OUR will, and ask for the strength and courage to become willing to forget resentments and false pride and make amends to those we have harmed. We must not do this step grudgingly, or as an unpleasant task to be rid of quickly. We must do it WILLINGLY, fairly and humbly, without condescension.

STEP No. 9—*Made direct amends to such people wherever possible, except when to do so would injure them or others."*

1. Here is where we make peace with ourselves by making peace with those we have hurt.

2. The amends we make must be direct. We must pay in kind for the hurt we have done them.

3. If we have cheated we must make restitution, except when to do so would injure others.

4. If we have hurt their feelings we must ask forgiveness from them.
5. The list of harms done may be long but the list of amends is equally as long.
6. For every *wrong* we have done, there is a *right* we may do to compensate.

There is only one exception. We must develop a sense of justice, a spirit of fairness, an attitude of common sense. If our effort to make amends would create further harm or cause a scandal, we will have to skip the *direct amends* and clean the matter up under STEP 5.

STEP No. 10—*Continued to personal inventory and when we were wrong, promptly admitted it.* In coming into AA we usually will have a pretty big inventory to work on, as in Steps 4, 8, 9. But, even after that, we will not be perfect. We have a long way to go. We will continue to make mistakes and will be inclined to do some more wrong thinking and wrong doing.

So, at intervals, we CONTINUE to take inventory. Here the purpose is to check on our progress. We certainly cannot be perfect so the need for regular inventory is apparent.

These inventories are PERSONAL. We confine the inventory to ourselves. We are the one who needs it. Never mind the other fellow. He, too, is probably troubled and will have to make his own inventory.

When we make these inventories, probably the best way to start is to go over, one by one, each of the twelve steps and try to discover just what, in these steps, we are not following.

The businessman HAS to make a physical inventory from time to time.

We have to make a personal inventory from time to time.

We have to make a personal inventory of ourselves from time to time if we want to recover from a serious mental illness.

So much for the Inventory Steps. Now look at some of the things we would do well to cover in an inventory.

1. Selfishness, the common vice of all alcoholics.
2. Egotism, who is without some of it? Self-importance. Mr. Big.

3. False pride, too big to admit a fault or an error.
4. Impatience, the spoiled child in a grown man.
5. Resentments, an Alcoholic usually is sore at the whole
6. Lack of Common Honesty, usually fooling ourselves and
7. Deceit.
8. Hate, the outgrowth of anger and resentment.
9. Jealousy, just *wanting* what the other fellow worked to get.
10. Envy, a sure-fire cause of discontent and unhappiness.
11. Self-pity, looking for sympathy when troubles are of your own making.
12. Uncontrollable temper, a sure sign of immaturity.
13. Sexual maladjustments which certainly require thorough covering in your personal inventory.
14. Laziness, just plain laziness.
—And so on through a long list.

Conversely, our inventory could show a list of virtues we very definitely lack, and should go to work on to develop, such as:

Honesty, Simple Justice, Fairness, Generosity, Truthfulness, Humility, Simplicity, Patience, Honest pride in work well done, Industry (to go to work and really work), Develop a sense of humor to combat temper tantrums and emotional upsets, Learn to laugh at yourself and situations, and so on through a long list.

Then consider a few major virtues.

Faith—If we have lost faith we must work desperately hard to get it back. Ask GOD to give us faith in HIM, our fellowman and ourselves.

Hope—If we have lost hope we are dead pigeons. Only those who have been cruelly hurt and in desperate need can know the wonderful sense of security that lies in hope for better things.

Trust—Since our own self-sufficient conduct of our own life has failed us, we must put our trust in GOD, who has never failed.

Meetings Number 4, 8, 12.

THIS MEETING COVERS THE TWELFTH STEP

Having had a spiritual experience as the result of these steps, we tried to carry this message to other alcoholics, and to practice these principles in all our affairs.

This STEP logically separates into three parts.

1. The SPIRITUAL EXPERIENCE

The terms *spiritual experience* and *spiritual awakening* used here and in the book ALCOHOLICS ANONYMOUS, mean, upon careful reading, that the personality change sufficient to bring about recovery from alcoholism has manifested itself among us in many forms.

Do NOT get the impression that these personality changes or spiritual experiences, must be in the nature of sudden and spectacular upheavals. Happily for everyone, this conclusion is erroneous.

Among our rapidly growing membership of thousands of alcoholics, such transformations, though frequent, are by no means the rule. Most of our experiences are what psychologist William James calls the *educational variety* because they develop slowly over a period of time. Quite often friends of the newcomer are aware of the difference long before he is himself.

The new man gradually realizes that he has undergone a profound alteration in his reaction to life; that such a change could hardly have been brought about by himself alone. What often takes place in a few months could seldom have been accomplished by years of self-discipline. With few exceptions our members find that they have tapped an unsuspected inner resource which they presently identify with their own conception of a Power greater than ourselves.

Most emphatically we wish to say that any alcoholic capable of honestly facing his problem in the light of our experience can recover, provided he does not close his mind to all spiritual concepts. He can only be defeated by an attitude of intolerance or belligerent denial.

We find that no one need have difficulty with the spiritual side of the Program. Willingness, honesty and open mindedness are the essentials of recovery and are the indispensable tools of a rich, successful experience.

2. CARRY THE MESSAGE TO OTHERS

This is the step of gratitude; it means exactly what it says. Carry the message actively. Bring it to the man who needs it. We do it in many ways.

a. By attending EVERY meeting of our own group.
b. By making calls when asked. Put your name on the available list.
c. By speaking at group meetings when asked.
d. By supporting our group financially to make group meetings possible.
e. By assisting at meetings when asked.
f. By setting a good example of complete sobriety.
g. By owning, and loaning to new members, our own copy of the big AA book.
h. By encouraging those who find the way difficult.
i. By serving as an officer or on group committees or special assignment when asked.
j. By doing all of the foregoing cheerfully and willingly.
k. We do any or all of the foregoing at some sacrifice to OURSELVES WITH DEFINITE THOUGHT OF DEVELOPING unselfishness in our own character.

3. WE PRACTICE THESE PRINCIPLES IN ALL OUR AFFAIRS. This last part of the TWELFTH STEP is the real purpose that all of the twelve steps lead to a new *way of life, a design for living.* It shows how to live right, think right and to achieve happiness.

HOW DO WE GO ABOUT IT?

a. We resolve to live our life, one day at a time, just twenty-four hours.
b. We pray each day for guidance that day.
c. We pray each night, thanks for that day.
d. We are patient.
e. Now, and most important, whatever LITTLE ordinary situation as well as BIG situations arise, we look at it calmly and fairly, with an open mind. Then act on it in exact accordance with the simple true principles that AA has taught and will teach us.

In other words, our SOBRIETY is only a correction of our worst and most evident faults. Our living each day according to the principles of AA will also correct all of our other lesser faults and will gradually eliminate, one by one, all of the defects in our character that cause frictions, discontents, and unhappy rebellious moods that lead right back to our very chief fault of drinking.

REFERENCES

1. Anonymous: *Alcoholics Anonymous*. New York: Alcoholic Anonymous World Services, Inc., 1955.
2. Anonymous: *Alcoholics Anonymous Comes of Age*. New York: Alcoholic Anonymous Publishing, Inc., 1957.
3. Mann, Marty: *New Primer on Alcoholism*. New York: Holt, Rinehart and Winston, 1966, p. 154.
4. Maxwell, Milton A.: *Professional and Alcoholic Anonymous Relations in Oregon: An Exploratory Study Report*. State of Oregon Mental Health Division, Alcohol Studies and Rehabilitation Section.
5. Mullan, H., and Sangiuliano, I.: *Alcoholism Group Psychotherapy and Rehabilitation*. Springfield, Illinois, Charles C Thomas.
6. W., William: The Society of Alcoholics Anonymous. *Am J Psychi*, **106** (5), November, 1949.

CHAPTER XIII

THOUGHTS TO OURSELVES

GEORGE STAUB
LEONA KENT

THE ONLY PROFESSIONAL who will stop for a drunk on the street is a policeman . . .

❉   ❉   ❉   ❉   ❉

Professionals are usually very willing to give up their prerogative at 10 o'clock at night . . .

❉   ❉   ❉   ❉   ❉

Dedication is good, but dedication with pay is better . . .

❉   ❉   ❉   ❉   ❉

For a professional to work well with a para-professional, he must be sure of his own talents . . .

❉   ❉   ❉   ❉   ❉

Sometimes, staffs consider their own growth more important than that of the client . . .

❉   ❉   ❉   ❉   ❉

There is no way to teach warmth . . .

❉   ❉   ❉   ❉   ❉

Being a recovered alcoholic neither qualifies nor disqualifies someone from helping a person with a drinking problem . . .

❉   ❉   ❉   ❉   ❉

Some professionals are unwilling to learn about self-help groups, yet they expect the para-professional to learn about professional methods . . .

❉   ❉   ❉   ❉   ❉

Alcoholics are like quicksilver—they can slip through your

fingers if you're not available to see them when the time is right . . .

*   *   *   *   *

There are fleeting moments during an alcoholic's drinking when he thinks about stopping. It's important to be available to him during these moments . . .

*   *   *   *   *

How difficult it must be for some trained and experienced professionals to acknowledge that para-professionals might actually determine the outcome of their treatment efforts . . .

*   *   *   *   *

Some people think that a career in alcoholic rehabilitation has low status, but we've always found it quite the opposite . . .

*   *   *   *   *

Professionals have the luxury of developing slowly in the sheltered environment of the classroom—para-professionals often have to swim . . . or sink . . .

*   *   *   *   *

Trying to develop good working relationships with professionals while being exploited is a painful process. Unlike the professional whose credentials automatically give him a card into the union, the para-professional must *prove* himself before he will be accepted into the union on a peer level . . .

*   *   *   *   *

The most important ingredient for an effective treatment team is mutual respect . . .

*   *   *   *   *

My personal experience leads me to believe that the key person in the growth and development of a para-professional is the program director. It is his support, encouragement and trust which motivates the para-professional to tap his own resources and develop his maximum potential . . .

*   *   *   *   *

Have you ever noticed that some alcoholism personnel preach abstinence but condone their own drunkenness . . .

*   *   *   *   *

What is there to be gained from proving that the professional is better qualified to serve the alcoholic—or from proving that it takes an alcoholic to help an alcoholic—*what* is being done is more important than *who* is doing it . . .

* * * * *

A para-professional once told us, "It often seemed to me that during normal working hours between eight and five, just speaking to a troubled client was interpretated as *counseling* and something I was not qualified to do, but between 5 p.m. and 10 p.m., speaking to a troubled client was called 'crisis intervention' and this was acceptable." . . .

* * * * *

Every new program is 125 percent successful in its first year . . .

* * * * *

When the counselor plays God, who gets crucified? . . .

* * * * *

Para-professionals need status, decent salary, opportunity for advancement—just like real people . . .

* * * * *

Para-professionals are people . . .

* * * * *

Para-professionals are real people . . .

* * * * *

I wonder if Bill W. was a para-professional . . .

* * * * *

Sometimes we think everyone else in the world has special talents except us . . .

* * * * *

I'm reminded of the time when I heard four professionals outline what they considered to be necessary qualifications for a para-professional. One was looking for an individual who was versatile . . . *able to make a pot of coffee and also able to address students in a classroom.* Another wanted a person *to wash the dirty diapers.* The third wanted someone to be available for any task at any time of the day or night and the fourth stated that he was looking for someone to work with him, side by side . . .

* * * * *

I hate the word *para-professional* . . . but it is better than *sub-professional* or *non-professional* . . .

* * * * *

Some recovered alcoholics scare me—they're so sure they know the answers . . .

* * * * *

Some professionals scare me too . . .

* * * * *

It always amazes us that other people see things differently than we do—especially when we're right . . .

* * * * *

Often times, people create a career ladder leading to professional status because they think it's better to be a professional than a para-professional . . .

* * * * *

When I hear some one say, "He looks like an alcoholic," I wonder what he means . . .

* * * * *

I have heard of an on-the-job para-professional training program which required that the para-professional take an oath of honesty each morning . . .

* * * * *

Since there is no scarcity of alcoholics, why is there so much bickering about who can do the best job of helping them . . .

* * * * *

Money alone does not make a good alcoholism program . . .

* * * * *

All treatment people should be allowed an albatross. In some cases one instinctively knows there is absolutely nothing that can be done to help someone get well, but you want to do it anyway . . .

* * * * *

A good way to lose friends and patients is to deplore the evils of drink . . .

* * * * *

I often say, "There but for the grace of God go I," when I

hear a recovered alcoholic say, "There but for the grace of God go I"...

＊　＊　＊　＊　＊

Those alcoholism personnel who drink should be prepared to be a model of self-discipline or the precepts which they advocate lose credibility...

＊　＊　＊　＊　＊

Those alcoholism personnel who do not drink should not set themselves up as judges of other peoples drinking behavior...

＊　＊　＊　＊　＊

Interest and motivation to help alcohoilcs is more important than formal training...

＊　＊　＊　＊　＊

I think one of the most important things to remember in working with alcoholics, is that it's okay to make a mistake. I find that the alcoholic almost always waits for me to correct it...

＊　＊　＊　＊　＊

How threatening it must be for some professionals who have worked hard and long to get their degrees, only to find out the para-professional can do an excellent job without one...

＊　＊　＊　＊　＊

In the early days the only time I felt confident was when I was with the client. The moment he left I was unsure. Without the support of the professional staff, I am certain I would have been unable to function in a professional setting. This support was not forthcoming immediately. It had to be earned ...

＊　＊　＊　＊　＊

Some professionals who have achieved top of the ladder success often have a para-professional at the bottom steadying the ladder...

＊　＊　＊　＊　＊

The one dispensable member of the treatment team is too often the alcoholic...

＊　＊　＊　＊　＊

At what stage does the para-professional become a professional in the eyes of the professional...

＊　＊　＊　＊　＊

At what stage does the para-professional become a professional in his own eyes . . .

❋   ❋   ❋   ❋   ❋

Why do some clinics find it necessary to treat all alcoholics as if they are mentally ill . . .

❋   ❋   ❋   ❋   ❋

We deplore labels. They make it seem like all alcoholics are the same, when in fact, they may have only one thing in common —they drink too much . . .

❋   ❋   ❋   ❋   ❋

For years alcoholics have been considered sick, and for even more years alcoholism has been considered a sin, but through sick and sin alcoholics and alcoholism have prevailed . . .

❋   ❋   ❋   ❋   ❋

AUTHOR INDEX

SUBJECT INDEX

A